A NEW DAY DAWNS

31 CHRISTMAS DEVOTIONS FOR DECEMBER

JOSHUA HERSHEY

Jubilee
Press · Promotions · Productions

A New Day Dawns
Copyright © 2021 Joshua Hershey
Published by Jubilee
All rights reserved.
ISBN: 978-1-7344241-1-9

CONTENTS

Forward

Toward the end of November 2020 one of the members of my church asked if I was planning on doing anything for Advent. I told him I was not. But soon after that discussion I decided I wanted to write a series of daily devotions for the church. (Thanks for stirring me to do something, Nef!) Every Monday through Saturday until Christmas I released a five hundred word devotion that had either an Advent or Christmas theme to it. Twenty-one in total.

Soon after completing the devotions I believed they might make a helpful Christmas book people could revisit each year. So during the last week of December 2020 and the month of December 2021 I wrote ten additional devotions, worked on editing all thirty-one, and pieced them together into the book you now hold in your hands.

Forcing myself to fit each devotion into four pages was a challenge. Every aspect of the Christmas story deserves far more attention than it is given here. While these reflections are *far from exhaustive* they are meant to be *somewhat extensive*. Meaning, I have attempted to cover the entirety of the infancy narratives in Matthew and Luke within these pages. The first twenty-five devotions are largely the infancy narratives in chronological order. The last six devotions delve into some of the ways the church has thought about Christmas through the centuries. I pray these devotions stir your imagination and serve as stepping stones for deeper reflection into the Greatest Story Ever Told!

The best way to read each devotion is with an open Bible in one hand and this book in the other. Begin by reading the Scripture that is listed in blue right below the title of each devotion. Then say a short prayer and thank the Lord for His Word. Finally, read the devotion. In all this should take about ten minutes each day.

The night Jesus Christ was born was truly special. It was nothing short of the dawning of a new day in history. Nothing would ever be the same again!

Joshua Hershey,
December 26th 2021

December 1st
A NEW DAY DAWNS
(LUKE 1:5-9)

The Christmas story opens with an elderly couple—Zechariah and Elizabeth. Both were descendants of Aaron. Both were devout in their faith and are described as "righteous before God" and "blameless." Luke also makes sure to mention that Zechariah was "of the division of Abijah" (Luke 1:5).

That last detail is significant. In 1 Chronicles we are told of the meticulous attention David pays to the organization of his budding kingdom (which in many ways is a type of Christ's kingdom). Portions of the *divine blueprint* David put in place were intact until the temple's destruction in AD 70—part of which entailed setting apart twenty-four priestly families to serve fortnightly shifts once a year in the temple. Each family's name, and the number of their shift, was written down for posterity. David's scribe Shemaiah wrote, "the eighth [shift] to Abijah" (1 Chr. 24:10).

Nearly one thousand years later Zechariah (a name meaning "Yahweh Remembers") was chosen to burn incense in the temple while serving Abijah's shift. He was serving during a season of history in which God had been 'canonically silent' for over four centuries. Meaning, God had not spoken a word of Holy Scripture *for a very long time.* But when God does begin to speak something that would become part of His enduring Word again, He chooses to do so to a priest named "Yahweh remembers" during the shift of Abijah—*the eighth shift.* Why? Partly because eight is the biblical number of new creation. As we read the story of Zechariah and Elizabeth, we are meant to recognize that what is about to happen is nothing less than the dawning of new creation on a *groaning, barren, dying,* and *wordless* world. But though things *appeared bleak,* God had *not forgotten His promises! He is the God who remembers. He is Zechar-YAH. Mindful-YAH.*

Think of how Elizabeth is described. She is said to be "well advanced in years" and "barren" (Luke 1:7). She is a perfect picture of humanity in need of a *new creation miracle*. She is beyond natural help and fully dependent on God's mercy if her and Zechariah's lineage is to continue. She could have chosen to be bitter about her state. But instead she is described as *righteous* and *blameless*. To be "righteous" means she had faith in the Lord and trusted Him regardless of her circumstances. She knew that God at times works mysteriously in ways we don't fully understand or prefer. In a similar manner to how God worked behind the scenes with Joseph for 13 years in Egypt, preparing to use him mightily, so God was working behind the scenes in Elizabeth and Zechariah's life. And they *trusted* Him. He was not only utilizing their lives for faithful service to others during their season of barrenness, but was also preparing their lives to be a witness of His amazing grace that was about to be poured out upon the *aging* and *barren* world.

The miracle God was about to work in the life of Elizabeth was a miracle of the same order as Sarah. Sarah also was "well advanced in years." Paul said she had a "dead womb" (Rom. 4:19). But nothing is too dead for Yahweh! He is the God who "who gives life to the dead and calls those things which do not exist as though they did" (Rom. 4:17). He is the God who comes to an *aging* and *barren* world with His eternal youthfulness and fruitfulness. In many ways Zechariah and Elizabeth are a new Abraham and Sarah—a father and mother of faith for those who were *patiently waiting* for the advent of new creation life. A father and mother of faith for those who *believe* Yahweh always remembers His promises!

This Christmas let us be like Zechariah. Priests of the eighth order declaring that new creation has dawned on our dying and barren world. Priests firmly convinced that Yahweh remembers His promises. Let us also be like Elizabeth. People of faith who trust the Lord in every season of life. People confident that God is always working behind the scenes. For we know God "works all things together for the good of those who love Him" (Rom. 8:28, NIV). Whether we are young like Mary and Joseph, or old like Elizabeth and Zechariah, God wants to use people from every age bracket to further His purposes. We simply need to 'show up' and 'be ready', like righteous Zechariah and Elizabeth.

"You are a chosen generation, a royal priesthood, a holy nation, His own special people, that you may proclaim the praises of Him who called you out of darkness into His marvelous light!" ~ 1 Peter 2:9

December 2nd
GABRIEL'S RETURN
(LUKE 1:8-25, 59-66)

While Zechariah was burning incense in the temple "an angel of the Lord appeared to him" (Luke 1:11). The Christmas narrative is *crammed full of angels*. This particular angel went on to declare how Zechariah and Elizabeth would bear a son who would be named "John" (Luke 1:13). He would be a Nazarite who would be "filled with the Spirit from the womb" and would go forth "in the power of Elijah" to make the people "ready for the Lord" (Luke 1:15-17).

Upon hearing this wondrous yet bewildering news, Zechariah asked *how* the birth of the child would take place seeing he and his wife were so old. The angel thundered back, "I am Gabriel. I stand in the presence of God, and I have been sent to speak to you and to tell you this good news" (Luke 1:19). Zechariah was not met by just *any* angel. This was the mighty Gabriel! The angel of greatest renown who stands in God's very presence. The angel who "flew with haste" to Daniel nearly half a millennia earlier and had disclosed *the heavenly timeline* concerning the coming of the Messiah (Dan. 9:20-27). It is *this mighty angel* who appeared to Zechariah as history was entering "the fulness of time" (Gal. 4:4)—*the end of the 490 year timeline Gabriel had prophesied about* (Dan. 9:24).

Because Zechariah did not simply receive the message from Gabriel, but exhibited some level of doubt, God made him mute (Luke 1:19-20). This divine pedagogy is something we can all appreciate. When doubt tries to creep in it is healthy to seal our lips from speaking unbelief and solely heed the heavenly word. For God's Word *always* comes true at its "appointed time" (Luke 1:20). No matter how improbable it sounds, it need *never* be questioned or doubted. "Only believe" (Mark 5:36).

One thing Gabriel was adamant about was that the child be named "John" (Luke 1:13). Why couldn't he be named Zechariah like all the family wanted? Would it really matter if we had 'Zechariah the Baptist' instead of 'John the Baptist'? Well, names are important to God. The last martyr in the Hebrew Bible was the prophet Zechariah (2 Chr. 24:22). This is one reason why Jesus said the corrupt Jewish leadership of His day would be held responsible for "the blood of Abel to the blood of Zechariah" (Luke 11:51). Zechariah's name *represented the end of the Old Testament era.* But God was wanting to do something new! A new name was right, fitting, and from God's point of view, *necessary.*

John was a 'pivot point' in history. His life represents the bridge from an era of promised mercy and grace (which is what the name Zechariah signifies) to an age of fulfilled mercy and grace (which is what the name John signifies). John is the best-man grinning from ear-to-ear as one-by-one his disciples leave his ministry and fall into the arms of Jesus (John 3:29). *He will gladly be that bridge.* He will gladly transition people from the old to the new!

John's name means "Yahweh has been gracious." Gabriel told Zechariah his child *must* be named that. The waiting world did not need another Zechariah. They did not need another promise, another prophet who reminded them of God's silence over the centuries. Rather, they needed to know that the fullness of God's promise *had arrived.* They needed to know the waiting was over, the kingdom was at hand, and the super-abundant grace of a new day had dawned! The beloved disciple says in his Gospel prologue, "the law was given through Moses, but grace and truth came through Jesus Christ" (John 1:17). John was the herald of this abounding grace!

If we can't enthusiastically say "amen" to God's Word, it's best to remain silent. God had to shut the mouth of Zechariah's doubt. In a similar way, let us refuse to give doubt space to mature this Christmas season. Instead, let's rest in His Word and be in awe of His grace. And in that environment of silence and rest let's allow God to 'drive the dark of doubt away'!

"We also have the prophetic message as something completely reliable, and you will do well to pay attention to it, as to a light shining in a dark place, until the day dawns and the morning star rises in your hearts." ~ 2 Peter 1:19, NIV

December 3rd
THE ANNUNCIATION
(LUKE 1:26-38)

Six months after appearing to the elderly Zechariah and announcing the miraculous birth of John, the angel Gabriel was sent to the young virgin Mary to announce *an even greater miraculous birth*. Upon entering her dwelling, Gabriel declared, "Rejoice, highly favored one, the Lord is with you; blessed are you among women" (Luke 1:28). Gabriel proceeded to tell Mary how she would conceive and bring forth a son named Jesus. Jesus means "salvation." Though

John was the greatest man born among women, this son would be *far greater* than John. He "will be great, and will be called the Son of the Highest; and the Lord God will give Him the throne of His father David" (Luke 1:32).

God chose a virgin from the lower class who lived in the *despised city* of Nazareth to mother the Messianic King. Nathaniel famously asked, "Can anything good come out of Nazareth?" (John 1:46) Yes! Mary would be a loving Nazarene mother. She was with Jesus from His first cry the day He was born to His last cry as He hung from the cross (John 19:26). She also was one of the disciples gathered during the day of Pentecost when her Son sent the Spirit to His church from His kingly throne (Acts 1:14). I imagine she was a calming presence in that upper room teaching the disciples how to wait for the promise of God, *for she had waited before.* She was likely honored and looked to not just by the 120, but by the Twelve as well.

It is no accident Gabriel was sent. Mary would have known about Gabriel from the book of Daniel and had also likely heard the story of Gabriel visiting her cousin. She would be an important part of how God would fulfill Gabriel's prophecy in Daniel. She would be *the vessel that would carry God's promise to fruition.* She would *enflesh the Messianic Son of Man who would receive an everlasting throne.* But how? How could a virgin conceive? Gabriel gives us a glimpse into the mystery. He said, "the Holy Spirit will come upon you" and "the power of the Highest will overshadow you" (Luke 1:35). Just as the Spirit of God *hovered over* the dark primal waters before creation sprang into existence, *so the Spirit of God would hover over Mary's dark womb* (Gen. 1:1-2). That was all she needed to know! For she knew the Spirit makes *something* out of *nothing.*

After miraculously conceiving, the King dwelt in the dark of Mary's womb for nine months. She was like the ark of Noah. If you do a carefully study of the flood chronology in Genesis 6-8 you will find that Noah dwelt in a fully enclosed ark for nine months before opening the ark's window and looking out upon a newly formed world. Noah was a Second Adam, but Christ is the Last Adam. He is a life-giving Adam (1 Cor. 15:22). While Noah came out of the ark and offered sacrifices (Gen. 8:20), Christ came into the world declaring that His body would be the Sacrifice to end sacrifices (Heb. 10:5-14). He was Mary's little lamb whose fleece was white as snow. He was the *spotless* and *blemishless* Lamb who would make all who receive Him *spotless* and *blemishless* (Col. 1:22).

Gabriel's last word to Mary is, "For with God nothing will be impossible" (Luke 1:37). And she responded, "Behold the maidservant of the Lord! Let it be to me according to your word" (Luke 1:38). Mary became God's willing servant. She accepted a very difficult assignment. One that would involve shame and pain. Later she would be told a sword would "pierce her soul" (Luke 2:35). But at the same time she was "highly favored"/"highly graced" for this assignment. So what does she say? "Let it be to me!"

This Christmas, let us be like Mary. Regardless of how sensible God's word sounds, or how challenging His assignments feel, we must declare, "Let it be to me according to your word." And as we do, God will always supply the grace we need. Mary was "overshadowed" with the Spirit. Christians, on the other hand, have been "baptized/immersed" in that same Spirit! We can rest assured that God's grace/power is fully sufficient for us to walk in obedience to the entirety of His Word (2 Cor. 12:9). God is with us, we are highly favored, and there is no reason to fear. We too can be willing servants.

> "He did not waver at the promise of God through unbelief, but was strengthened in faith, giving glory to God, and being fully convinced that what He had promised He was also able to perform."
>
> ~ Romans 4:20-21

December 4th
JOHN'S LEAP FOR JOY
(LUKE 1:39–45)

Mary, being a cousin of Elizabeth, likely knew about the appearance of Gabriel to Zechariah announcing a similar miraculous birth, and how her elderly cousin was becoming great with child. So what does Mary do after her encounter with Gabriel? "She went to the hill country with haste… and entered the house of Zechariah" (Luke 1:39-40). She immediately packed her bags and bolted to the hill country! She knew Elizabeth would believe her story about a virgin conception and *encourage* her in her holy assignment. She knew she needed to be surrounded with a like-minded person of faith who was also bringing a promise of God to fruition. *We all need faith-filled friends and family on our journey who can stand with us and encourage us.*

"And it happened, when Elizabeth heard the greeting of Mary, that the babe leaped in her womb; and Elizabeth was filled with the Holy Spirit" (Luke 1:41). What happened in Zechariah and Elizabeth's little home was nothing short of a miniature Pentecost! It wasn't simply Mary, but the Holy Spirit Baptizer Himself, who entered that priestly home tucked away in the Judean hills. Though Jesus was just conceived, His presence caused Elizabeth (and John) to be *filled with the Holy Spirit*. Elizabeth broke out in praise and John began to dance. He danced like David danced before the ark of Lord—for in many ways Mary was like an 'ark of the Lord' herself (2 Sam. 6:16).

From the moment John encountered Jesus he was prepared for his heavenly assignment (Luke 1:15). Like Jeremiah, he was *called from his mother's womb* (Jer. 1:5). Like Samson, he was *a Nazarite from the womb* (Judg. 13:5). Samson's mother couldn't drink any wine or strong drink while she was pregnant because that would in turn feed the unborn Nazarite child (Judg. 13:4). The matriarch, Rebekah, was told by the Lord "two nations are in your womb" (Gen. 25:23). *Heavenly assignments begin at conception.* Our unique personalities and giftings begin developing the moment our parent's chromosomes unite and the spark of God's life calls us into being. The One at work *unlocking* genes, *crafting* personalities, *calling forth* limbs and organs, and *causing* us to dream, kick, and dance in the womb is our All Wise Creator and Assignment Maker.

The stories of Jacob, Esau, Jeremiah, Samson, John, and Jesus all highlight the *sacred personhood of children in the womb.* The child in the womb is a living being who is carefully woven together by our Heavenly Father (Psalm 139). The child in the womb is *not* the mother's body, *not* the mother's tissue which can be 'discarded' if one likes. Rather, the child is a *separate* and *sacred human* who *bears God's image and likeness* (James 3:9). To 'abort' the unborn is murder. To stop a beating heart and "shed innocent blood" is one of the "seven things the Lord hates" (Prov. 6:17). Christmas teaches us that all children are important and sacred to the Lord, *especially children in the womb.*

They too can dance and sing. Let us bring the unborn before the presence of the Lord this Christmas and allow them to enter the full joys of their Savior!

After John settled down, Elizabeth declared, "Blessed are you among women, and blessed is the fruit of your womb! ... Blessed is she who believed, for there will be a fulfillment of those things which were told her from the Lord" (Luke 1:42, 45). Mary was seeking encouragement, and she found it!

We are called to be like Mary this Christmas. To believe and receive His Word. To seek encouragement and to encourage others. The book of Hebrews instructs us to "imitate those who through faith and patience inherit the promises" (Heb. 6:12). Imitating the faith of Mary is a great place to start. If we imitate Mary we will certainly have a Merry Christmas. We too are an 'ark of the Lord'. We too 'carry His presence' to others (1 Cor. 3:16). We too can cause others to leap with joy. When Paul and Silas were singing in their chains at midnight the entire prison population was listing to them and "everyone's chains were loosed" (Acts 16:26). Paul and Silas knew they were like Mary. They brought Christ into the dark dungeon cells and dancing liberation ensued!

"Rejoice in the Lord always. Again I will say, rejoice!" ~ Philippians 4:4

18

December 5th
THE MAGNIFICAT
(LUKE 1:46-56)

After being told how blessed she was by both Gabriel and Elizabeth, Mary broke out in song. This song, generally known by its Latin name, *The Magnificat*, was no sugary nursery rhyme. Rather, it was a heartfelt declaration of gratitude for the God of mercy *and justice*. Mary knew that to be the carrier of the Messiah meant she was carrying the One who would turn the world inside-out. The Messiah would pull down the powerful and uplift the humble (Luke 1:52). The Messiah would fill the hungry with good things and send the rich away empty (Luke 1:53). Mary believed God was about to rain down "righteousness like a mighty stream" (Amos 5:24).

It is important to be aware that the name "Mary" is the same name as "Miriam." In Greek her name is Μαριάμ. Well, what do we know about Miriam from Scripture? We first meet her *keeping watch over a baby* who would deliver Israel from the land of slavery (Ex. 2:4). But what she is primarily known for is being the first woman to *break out in song* in the Bible. After Pharaoh's army was drowned in the Red Sea Miriam led the dancing women of Israel with a timbrel in her hand as they sang, "Sing to the Lord, for he is highly exalted. Both horse and driver he has hurled into the sea" (Ex. 15:21).

Miriam sang a song of deliverance! A song celebrating God's mercy and justice! Her role in song and dance was of no small importance in the Lord's redemption of Israel. The Lord reminded His people in Micah, "I sent Moses, Aaron, and Miriam to help you" (Mic. 6:4). How did Miriam help Israel? She helped them learn how to praise the Lord. She taught them that we are saved *to sing*. We are delivered *to dance*. We set free *to be saturated in the Spirit* and forever *give thanksgiving and praise*.

Mary's song in Elizabeth's home is sung in the same key as Miriam's. She was confident the fruit of her womb would be the Messianic King of Psalm 2 who would break the wicked leaders in the world "with a rod of iron" and "dash them to pieces like pottery" (Ps. 2:9). The horse and rider will be drowned in the sea, *again*. As Mary puts it, "He has shown strength with His arm; He has scattered the proud in the imagination of their hearts. He has put down the mighty from their thrones" (Luke 1:51-52).

While Mary sings in *the key* of Miriam, her *actual lyrics* closely parallel the beautiful song of Hannah (1 Sam. 2:1-10). These women knew that God *comes down to deliver the oppressed* (Ex. 3:8; Ps. 18:9; Dan. 6:27). They knew He is a God who is *faithful to His covenants* (Luke 1:55). They knew God especially *cares about the lowly, humble, poor, and hungry* (1 Sam. 2:5, 7-8; Luke 2:48, 52-53). They knew God *deals with tyrants and oppressors* (1 Sam. 2:4, 10; Luke 2:52). We must rest in the truth that God's Son, His appointed King, *will have the last word over all of the world's tragedies* (Ps. 2; Rev. 11:15).

The baby born of Mary was not the sweet and mild Child we tend to see in religious art. *While Jesus was kind, tender, and compassionate, He also was a Messianic Warrior.* He was born in a world taken captive by sin

21

and death. A world under the sway of the wicked dragon of old who sought to devour Mary and seeks to devour us (Rev. 12). John wrote that the Messiah "was manifested in order to destroy the works of the devil" (1 John 3:8). *Christ came to reverse the curse. To deceive the deceiver. To smash the serpent's head.* A 'Greater Exodus' came about with the entrance of Christ into the world. An Exodus from the slavery of the dark powers of Sin and Satan—two spiritual powers that had deeply embedded themselves in humanity and left us hopeless. Jesus, the Greater Moses, the Son of the Highest, came to "set the captive free" (Luke 4:18). Mary knew this. This is why she burst out in song like Miriam of old.

Mary opened her song with, "My soul magnifies the Lord, And my spirit has rejoiced in God my Savior" (Luke 1:46-47). This Christmas let us be like Mary. Let us magnify the Lord in song. Let us rejoice in all He has done to save and deliver. Just as Mary sang before Elizabeth so let us "admonish one another in psalms and hymns and spiritual songs" and "sing with grace in our hearts to the Lord" (Col. 3:16).

"Let them shout for joy and be glad, Who favor my righteous cause; And let them say continually, 'Let the LORD be magnified, Who has pleasure in the prosperity of His servant.'" ~ Psalm 35:27

December 6th
THE BENEDICTUS
(LUKE 1:67-80)

Every single written song in the entirety of the four Gospels is found in the Christmas narratives. In fact, all four of them are found in the infancy narrative in Luke. Besides these songs, there is a reference to Jesus and the disciples "singing a hymn" before they go to the garden of Gethsemane (Mark 14:26). But the only *written songs* in the Gospels are in Luke 1-2. One thing this signifies is that Christmas should be a season saturated with song!

Christians should joyously, triumphantly, and frequently sing the many wonderful Christmas carols that have been written over the centuries. While singing about 'chestnuts roasting over an open fire' or 'sleigh bells in the snow' is delightful and gives us appreciation for all of the Lord's wondrous gifts in nature, it is even more important to sing about the supernatural gift of Jesus. We must *hark* the *herald of the angels* as they *bend to earth* and *touch their harps of gold*. Our imaginations should expand as we meditate on the *holy night* of Christ's birth. Our hearts should be lifted up in a joyful state as we sing about the *Everlasting Light* who shines in the *dark streets* of *little Bethlehem*.

Carols about the birth of Jesus bring hope and light in a world that is often dejected and dark. Zechariah's song, his *Benedictus*, is one such carol. He sings triumphantly of God "visiting and redeeming His people", of God "raising up a horn of salvation", of God "remembering His covenant" and "performing the mercy promised the fathers" (Luke 1:69-72). It is a song of great thanksgiving for a God who makes good on His promises and acts on behalf of His people. The depth of many of these deep theological truths Zechariah sings about can in some ways only be captured by poetry and song. The Christmas season should be overflowing with poetry. For only poetry can fully capture the beauty, grandeur, and mystery of what God has done in Christ!

The end of the *Benedictus* is especially poetic in its portrayal of salvation. Zechariah sings about his son, John, who would go before Christ in order to "give his people the knowledge of salvation through the forgiveness of their sins, because of the tender mercy of our God, by which the rising sun will come to us from heaven to shine on those living in darkness and in the shadow of death, to guide our feet into the path of peace" (Luke 1:77-79).

Christmas is the dawning of a New Day. We celebrate the God of Light who came into our world in its deepest darkness. "Every good gift and every perfect gift is from above, and comes down from the Father of lights" (James 1:17). The Celestial Light, the Unending Day, shined with an intensity the world had not yet known when Jesus entered the world. For Jesus is the "brightness of God's glory" (Heb. 1:3). As the Light of the world and the Tender Mercy of God, Jesus met us in "the shadow of death" in order to bring us into new creation light. Christmas is good news for the sinful, the discouraged, the hopeless, and the forsaken. It is "good news" of "great joy" to "all people" (Luke 2:10). God has come. And, He loves us! One early church father who captured this truth so well was John Chrysostom. This golden-mouthed preacher declared, "Neither is there any other cause of the incarnation except this alone: He saw us bowed down to the ground, perishing, tyrannized by death; and He had mercy."[1]

The Daystar from on High has risen with healing in His wings (Mal. 4:2). The Eternal Light of God who gives light to the world entered the darkness of Mary's womb and subsequently the darkness of our world. "The light shines in the darkness, and the darkness has not overcome it" (John 1:5, NIV). This Christmas let us, like Zechariah, be grateful for this Merciful Light!

"Jesus took Peter, James, and John, and led them up on a high mountain apart by themselves; and He was transfigured before them. His clothes became shining, exceedingly white, like snow, such as no launderer on earth can whiten them. ... And a cloud came and overshadowed them; and a voice came out of the cloud, saying, 'This is My beloved Son. Hear Him!'" ~ Mark 9:2-3, 7

December 7th
A DREAMING JOSEPH
(MATTHEW 1:18-25)

The first time we meet a Joseph in Scripture what is he doing? Dreaming. Genesis 37 describes two God-given dreams of Joseph. Both were not well received by his brothers. In fact, they wanted to kill him! But ultimately they ended up selling him into slavery instead. Nevertheless, Joseph's dreams came true in due season. His brothers ended up bowing down before him as he rose to become the Prime Minister of Egypt. And Joseph's father, Jacob, and his entire family ended up moving to Egypt so they could escape a destructive famine in the land of Israel.

The Gospel of Matthew opens with a narrative about another dreaming Joseph. This Joseph also had a father named Jacob (Matt. 1:16). He also had many dreams (Matt. 1:20; 2:13, 19). He also led his family to the land of Egypt fleeing harm's way (Matt. 2:14). And his first dream occurred after receiving news that his betrothed wife, Mary, was pregnant through the power of the Holy Spirit.

Many people assume that Joseph was unaware that Mary had a supernatural conception. The common interpretation is that the reason he sought to divorce her was because she had committed adultery (or possibly was raped). And most English translations reflect that assumption. But an alternative way to read this story is that Joseph was fully aware that Mary had been impregnated by the Lord and the reason he considered annulling their contractural agreement before their coming betrothal was that he was unsure if he was part of God's plan in this great redemptive act.

On this reading, verse 19 should be translated, "Joseph, son of David, do not fear to take Mary your wife even though that which is conceived in her is indeed of the Holy Spirit." The angel is assuring Joseph that he is part of God's plan and has a God given vocation. He is addressed as "Joseph, son of David." The fact that he is of the *direct lineage* of David, and would be the *legal father* of Jesus, was of massive redemptive significance. (See Day 14 and Matt. 1:1-17). That alone was vocation worthy!

Before having been given the heavenly assurance through his dream Joseph was likely thinking, "Is it possible that I would be called to be the father of the Messiah? Should I even attempt to touch Mary? Remember what happened to Uzzah?!? I know many people will not believe the virgin birth story and might think Mary is worthy of death because she must have committed adultery. But I know that is not the case, and seeing I am righteous, maybe the best thing to do is to break off our coming betrothal quietly?" The purpose the heavenly dream was to assure him that he *was chosen* for the holy assignment of raising the Messiah and *was an essential part* of the holy family. God had *appointed* him for such a time as this! His dream also helped him understand how to defend that Mary was a virgin by Gabriel's reference to the *prophecy* of Isaiah (Matt. 1:24). So what does he do upon awaking? *He steps into his heavenly vocation.* He "took to him his wife" (Matt. 1:25).

Though Joseph likely experienced a season of scorn and ridicule, just like OT Joseph, he eventually would see beautiful confirmations of everything the angel told him in his dreams. The last time we hear of Joseph is when Jesus is twelve. Mary and Joseph were anxiously searching for him for three days after He was left behind in Jerusalem during Passover. Once they found Him in the temple, Jesus told them, "Why did you seek Me? Did you not know that I must be about My Father's business?" (Luke 2:49) This was no son of adultery, this was *the Son of the Heavenly Father.*

Though Joseph disappears from the biblical narrative after this, he witnessed the truth of what was announced to him 13 years earlier. Interestingly, the Old Testament Joseph began to see his dreams mature exactly 13 years after his dreams as well. God's prophetic dreams always come true in His own timing. This Christmas, let us be open to receive heavenly vocations for our lives. Let us be open to visions and dreams.

"In the last days, God says, I will pour out my Spirit on all people. Your sons and daughters will prophesy, your young men will see visions, your old men will dream dreams." ~ Acts 2:17, NIV

December 8th

THE JOURNEY TO BETHLEHEM

(LUKE 2:1-5)

The Holy Family's journey from Galilee to Bethlehem has captured the imagination of Christians for
centuries. Even today many tourists in Israel will
backpack the one hundred mile "Nativity Trail." The
journey includes all sorts of terrain from rocky
hillsides and desert valleys, to lush green olive groves
where hikers have opportunity to rest. While the *exact*

path Mary and Joseph followed can not be known for certain, we do know that it would have been quite the journey for a woman well into her pregnancy.

Their journey reminds me of the summer before my junior year of college when I backpacked a portion of the Appalachian Trail with my grandpa and younger cousin. In planning our trip we made one crucial mistake—by choosing to start in Harper's Ferry, West Virginia my grandpa was immediately met with the rocky and jagged terrain of western Maryland. Though this portion of the trail is only forty miles, it is absolutely miserable. In fact, my grandpa had to drop out sooner than expected. If we had instead started in Pennsylvania, where the trail was dirt and flat, my grandpa would have been able to continue the backpacking trip much longer.

The reason I bring this experience up is to remind us that Mary and Joseph's journey to Bethlehem was far from easy. Not only would the change of terrain and distance be a challenge for a pregnant woman, but there was always the possibility of encountering wild animals or thieves. So, why did Mary and Joseph make this difficult journey? Because "a decree went out from Caesar Augustus that all the world should be registered... So all went to be registered, everyone to his own city" (Luke 2:1-3). On a surface level Mary and Joseph's journey had to do with *government compliance*, but on a deeper level it had to do with God's *providential fulfillment of prophecy*.

Joseph journeyed "to the city of David, which is called Bethlehem, because he was of the house and lineage of David" (Luke 2:4). Micah had prophesied that the Christ would be born in Bethlehem. He said, "But you, Bethlehem Ephrathah, though you are little among the thousands of Judah, yet out of you shall come forth to Me the One to be Ruler in Israel, whose goings forth are from of old, from everlasting" (Mic. 5:2). This heavenly word could not be thwarted. Though Luke says the impetus for the journey was the decree of Caesar, ultimately, a far greater providential work was taking place.

There are seasons in every life when God is fulfilling His purposes even though the journey is difficult. In fact, those tend to be the times when God does His greatest work. History is His-story. God's invisible hand is at work in ways that many times are imperceptible in the moment. Think of Abraham leaving Ur and journeying to the Promised Land. The book of Hebrews says "he went out, not knowing where he was going" (Heb. 11:8). This would have been a difficult season leaving family, friends, and land behind. But ultimately God would exceedingly bless Abraham and make his name great (Gen. 24:1). Think of Joseph journeying through the slave and prison system of Egypt for thirteen years. Joseph could have been exceedingly angry at what was done to him by his brothers. But after rising to power and realizing that many lives would be saved because he held the position he did, Joseph could say to his brothers who sold him into slavery, "God sent me before you to preserve life" (Gen. 45:5).

God is always at work behind the scenes orchestrating events for His good and glorious purposes. We must not be discouraged by circumstances. Joseph and Mary could have been tempted to be upset by the census. But they didn't let the political frustrations overwhelm them. This Christmas let us be like Joseph and travel the road before us knowing God is with us. Let us be like Mary knowing Jesus indwells us. Even if we might be on a difficult part of the journey, know the Good Shepherd always leads His sheep 'through' the valley of the shadow of death 'into' green pastures and still waters (Ps. 23:2-4).

"And we know that all things work together for good to those who love God, to those who are the called according to His purpose."
~ Romans 8:28

December 9th

AWAY IN A MANGER

(LUKE 2:6-7)

"Away in a manger no crib for a bed, the little Lord Jesus lay down His sweet head." Many cherish this sweet Christmas carol. Especially when sung by children during a school or church Christmas program. But for many Christians, the significance of *why* Jesus had a manger as a bed, outside of Him being a poor child born in a stable, rarely crosses their minds. But the manger is *very important* to the Christmas story. In fact, Luke mentions it three times!

Sometime after Mary arrived in Bethlehem, Luke writes, "the time came for her to give birth. And she gave birth to her firstborn son and wrapped him in swaddling cloths and laid him in a manger, because there was no place for them in the inn" (Luke 2:6-7). A manger was the most comfortable place Mary could find for her newborn. The "inn", *in one sense a picture for the world at large*, had "no place" for Jesus. A large portion of those He came to "received Him not", "left Him", and demanded His crucifixion (John 1:11, 6:66, 19:6). The prophet Isaiah said He would be "despised and rejected by men" (Is. 53:3). This rejection began *the very day He was born.*

The level of discomfort and inconvenience Christ would experience mattered not to Him. He simply desired to be with us! To be Immanuel! And the fact that He had a manger—an animal feeding trough— as a crib is filled with prophetic significance. There is a reason it is mentioned *three times* (Luke 2:7, 12, 16). This detail is clearly of no small importance and God wants us to meditate upon it. The angels even say it would be a "sign" to the shepherds.

The English word "manger" comes from a French word which means "to eat." And the French word is built off of a Latin word which means "to chew." It is as if Jesus was placed on a dining table at birth. Presented as *the main course*. The suggestion that we can "dine on Jesus" becomes even clearer when we understand that Bethlehem means "the house of bread." The Hebrew word, *beth*, means "house." The word, *lehem*, means "bread." In the Gospel of John, Jesus declares, "I am the living bread which came down from heaven. If anyone eats of this bread, he will live forever; and the bread that I shall give is My flesh, which I shall give for the life of the world" (John 6:51). The 'Living Bread' came to the 'House of Bread' and was placed in the 'feeding trough' in order give His flesh for the life of the world!

Christmas is a season of feasting. Turkeys, tamales, casseroles, cookies, and fruit cakes fill our homes and bellies. This is all wonderful, and we should thank God when we have such material blessings in our lives, but we must especially remember to come to the manger at Christmas and *feast on Jesus*. Jesus must be the *main course*. We are what we eat. If we are feeding on Jesus and His Word, we will begin to reflect His life and character more and more. Instead of our bodies becoming more weighty, our spirits and souls will become weighty with the glory of God. This Feast is open for rich and the poor. For shepherd and magi. Anyone who will humble themselves, come out of the world's cluttered inn, and worship the despised and rejected One. Jesus said, "when you give a feast, invite the poor, the maimed, the lame, the blind. And you will be blessed, because they cannot repay you" (Luke 14:13-14). This is what Jesus has done for us!

Lastly, Luke records that Jesus was "wrapped in swaddling cloths." There is one other time Jesus was wrapped in cloths. After Jesus's body was taken down from the cross they "bound it in linen cloths" (John 19:40). Interestingly, many archaeologists believe the manger in Bethlehem was made of stone. So too was the tomb they laid Jesus in (Matt. 27:60).

His birth is a prophetic picture of His death. The 'sign' of the manger is that Jesus was born to die. In the stable, among the lowing ox and donkey (Is. 1:3), Christ is the Lamb. The "Lamb of God who takes away the sin of the world" (John 1:29). This Christmas let us feast on the Bread of Life and Lamb of God. Let us get on our knees, bow our heads, and humbly come before the Greater Passover who has saved us from Death by His Death in order to bring us Everlasting Life.

"Man shall not live by bread alone, but by every word that proceeds from the mouth of God."
~ Deuteronomy 8:3 & Matthew 4:4

December 10th

BECOMING FLESH

(JOHN 1:1-18)

John's Gospel does not contain an infancy narrative like Matthew and Luke. Instead, it contains a deep theological prologue concerning *who* the baby born on Christmas is. What began at the annunciation and came to fruition in Bethlehem was an unprecedented act of God. John writes, "In the beginning was the Word, and the Word was with God, and the Word was God... And the Word became flesh and dwelt among us, and we beheld His glory" (John 1:1, 14).

39

Jesus is none other than the Eternal Word, the Eternal Son of God, made flesh for our salvation. The Babe in the womb of Mary was none other than God's Word who spoke all things into existence. He is the Creator become creation. Though the Word has beginnings before all time, in the infinite recesses of eternity, He *entered time* and *became 'fleshly' man* in the womb of Mary. The Son of God became a first century Jew with all the 'fleshly entanglements' and 'societal structures' life at that time entailed. And while He *fully entered* our world, and was *fully man*, at the same time, the Babe in the manger never ceased to be anything other than Immanuel—*fully God with us* (Is. 7:14; Matt. 1:23).

John's prologue gives the basic building blocks for constructing a robust theology of *the person of Christ.* He is the God-Man. *Fully God* without impeding in any way His *full humanity.* It is the Word who "became flesh." In John's Gospel the "Word" is synonymous with the "Son" (John 1:18). John says the Word/Son *was* God and at the same time was *with* God (John 1:1). This is the grammar which undergirds the mystery of the triunity of God. A mystery revealed but not fully explained. A mystery we worship and relate to, more than fully intellectually unravel. *God simply is Father, Son, Spirit.* That is His name (Matt. 28:19). Not three gods. Not three separate wills or personalities. One God. But one God who exists as three eternal relations *mutually indwelling* one another.

The Father has never been without the Son. If He had, He would cease to be 'Father'. The Son has never been without the Father. If He had, He would cease to be 'Son'. The new thing that occurs at Christmas is not that the Son comes into existence, but rather, that the Eternal Son 'becomes' flesh. The God who dwelt behind the curtains, guarded by the flaming cherubim, makes entrance into our world through the womb of a virgin! He does so in order to forever bridge our sinful separation, give us life, and bring us back into full communion with Himself. He becomes *fleshly* so that we might become *heavenly*.

John ends his prologue, "No one has seen God at any time. The only begotten Son, who is in the bosom of the Father, He has declared Him" (John 1:18). Jesus makes God *more known* than ever before. Though God had revealed Himself through the prophets, and in diverse manners and ways before Christmas, in Christ "the radiance of God's glory and the exact representation of his being" shines forth (Heb. 1:3). Jesus is "the image of the invisible God" (Col. 1:15). Jesus is the clearest 'selfie' of God we possess.

The more we behold Christ with eyes of faith, the more the heart of God is brought into focus. Jesus said, "He who has seen Me has seen the Father" (John 14:9). There is no other God, no hidden God, no unrevealed God, behind the back of Jesus Christ. Read the Word, study the Gospels, meditate on the epistles, and do it all in light of the Word made flesh —Jesus.

This Christmas let us be grateful that the Eternal Son of God would humble Himself to become flesh and tabernacle among us (Phil. 2:8). To be bounded, suffer, and die that we might know Him and enter into abundant and eternal life. To fully enter our humanity to redeem it while simultaneously revealing the nature and character of God. Christ emphatically reveals that God is "for us and not against us" (Rom. 8:31). As God, He graciously meets us east of Eden in order to bring us back into the garden to be with Him forever.

"The Son of God has come and has given us understanding, so that we may know him who is true. And we are in him who is true by being in his Son Jesus Christ. He is the true God and eternal life." ~ John 5:20, NIV

December 11th

SHEPHERDS HEAR GLAD TIDINGS

(LUKE 2:8-20)

The night of Jesus' birth, in the fields surrounding Bethlehem, shepherds were "keeping watch over their flocks by night" (Luke 2:8). Of all the people God could have announced the birth of His Son to on this most glorious night, He chose a group of shepherds. It is important to note that shepherds in Jesus' day were despised by many. For various reasons, Jewish oral law referred to shepherds as "incompetent" and even said people "shouldn't help them out of a pit." Randy Alcorn writes, "In Christ's day, shepherds stood on the bottom rung of the Palestinian social ladder. They shared the same unenviable status as tax collectors and dung sweepers."[2]

God's *heavenly host—His massive angel army*—was sent to announce the news of the birth of the Messiah. And they were not sent to the highly refined rabbis and religious leaders a few miles away in Jerusalem, but rather to *the bottom rung of the social order watching sheep in the fields*. Upon being blinded by the glorious celestial light radiating from the angel of the Lord, and while likely quivering with fear, the angel said to the shepherds, "Do not be afraid, for behold, I bring you good tidings of great joy which will be to all people. For there is born to you this day in the city of David a Savior, who is Christ the Lord" (Luke 2:10-11).

All people? Did this heavenly ambassador really just include *everyone*? Even lowly and despised *shepherds*? Yes, he most certainly did! All means *all*. No one is excluded from the gift of salvation brought by Christ! In fact, Jesus especially made it a point in His earthly ministry to go to the margins of society. To eat with "tax collectors and sinners" (Matt. 9:10). To "touch the leper" (Matt. 8:3) To "forgive the sinner and adulterer" (Mark 2:5; John 8:11). To preach to the "Samaritan" (John 4:42). He said concerning Himself, "The Son of God has come to seek and save that which was lost" (Luke 19:10). On that Holy Night over two-thousand years ago a Savior was born for the rich and poor, old and young, educated and uneducated, slave and free, Jew and Gentile, sinner and chief of sinner. No one is excluded from the salvation of the Savior born in the city of David!

After the shepherds were stunned by this announcement, "suddenly there was with the angel a multitude of the heavenly host praising God and saying: 'Glory to God in the highest, And on earth peace, goodwill toward men!'" (Luke 2:13-14) The size of the angelic host in heaven is "ten thousand times ten thousand" (Ps. 68:17; Dan. 7:10; Rev. 5:11). That is 100,000,000 angels. A large portion of that army came to the field of Bethlehem to announce the birth of the King of heaven and earth. The entire sky was filled with angelic creatures from the highest heaven bursting with joy over what was transpiring in this little town. They longed to peer into the mysterious glories of this extravagant and inconceivable love (1 Pet. 1:12).

Edmund Sears beautifully captured this moment in his carols. He spoke of "angels bending near the earth, to touch their harps of gold" and "celestial choirs from courts above shedding sacred glories" on the fields of Judea. The veil between earth and heaven was being drawn back on this sacred night. And man, along with the all the groaning creation, was audience to heaven's triumphant song. The greatest Christmas concert ever performed!

In the new covenant, man has replaced angels in authority. We are no longer under those old covenant guardians. Man has also replaced them on their heavenly thrones (a theme in Revelation where we see twenty-four angels leave their thrones and twenty-four men take their place as the last judgment is brought on the harlot city Jerusalem in 70 AD). Christians are now the heavenly ambassadors of the King (2 Cor. 5:20). Recreated men now "shine as stars" and heavenize our world (Phil. 2:15). Let us sing with gusto and boldly announce good news of great joy about our Savior this Christmas! Let us shine bright as God's heavenly host, seated with Him in heavenly places!

> "You are the light of the world. ... Let your light so shine before men, that they may see your good works and glorify your Father in heaven."
> ~ Matthew 5:14, 16

December 12th

JESUS' GENEALOGY

(MATTHEW 1:1-17; LUKE 3:23-38)

"The book of the genealogy of Jesus Christ, the Son of David, the Son of Abraham" (Matt. 1:1). This is how the New Testament opens. God wants us to know that the story of Jesus is intricately connected to Israel's story. That it continues what God began when He chose Abram out of Ur and David from the eight sons of Jesse. Mary and Joseph were not randomly chosen either. They were both direct descendants of

David and Abraham. Their child has a legal right to be king and reign forever (2 Sam. 7:12-16).

There are two genealogies for Jesus. Matthew's genealogy highlights God's covenantal faithfulness to Israel and records Christ's line through Joseph. A line which descends from David's son Solomon (Matt. 1:6). Luke's genealogy highlights God's universal redemption and records Jesus' lineage all the way back to Adam (likely) through Mary. Mary's line went through David's son Nathan (Luke 3:31). *Two direct lines to David.* A double stamp of approval! The Risen and Reigning Christ appears in Revelation declaring, "I am the Root and the Offspring of David, the Bright and Morning Star" (Rev. 22:16). The genealogies of Jesus prove this declaration of the Risen Christ beyond a shadow of a doubt.

Matthew's genealogy is divided into three sets of 14 (Matt. 1:17). Fourteen is the gematrial value of David (דוד). That means the numerical values of the Hebrew letters of 'David' add up to 14. David is also the fourteenth son in the genealogy. He is central to the entire structure of Christ's genealogy for Christ's birth is the fulfillment of God's covenant to David that he would have a son who would reign forever (something that regularly comes up in the infancy narratives of both Matthew and Luke). The three sets of 14 equals 42 generations in all. 42 is the gematrial value of Jubilee (יבל). (Authors of Scripture regularly use gematria. The original audience would have been very familiar with this common literary device.)

Jubilee is the biblical 'super sabbath'. It happens after seven seven-year cycles on the fiftieth year. This 'super year' did not simply include physical rest, but economic rest and peace were also returned to the people (Lev. 25). It was cause for great jubilation! At the end of His first sermon Jesus declared that He came to "set at liberty those who are oppressed" and "proclaim the acceptable year of the Lord" (Luke 4:18-19). The advent of Jesus means the beginning of a Jubilee. It means a super abundance of *rest, restoration,* and *renewed inheritance* has arrived!

According to the book of Chronicles, Cyrus was the 50th generation from Adam. He set the Babylonian captives free to go back to their land, and funded their new building project. Jesus is the Greater Cyrus. He might not be the 50th from Adam, but He follows the 'gematrial jubilee' in the 42nd position from Abraham and brings about the greatest Jubilee the world has ever known as the Seed of Abraham. This Greater Cyrus rescues us from bondage to sin and calls us to "go into all the world" and be vessels building His church (Matt. 28:18-20). Like Cyrus, He abundantly supplies what we need from His own resources for this building project (Ezra 1:1-4; John 15:1-5; Phil. 4:19).

Lastly, Matthew's genealogy is unique in that it includes *four women*—Tamar, Rahab, Ruth, and Bathsheba. One thing this points to is *Gentile inclusion*. Tamar and Rahab were Canaanites. Ruth was a Moabite. Bathsheba was married to a Hittite.

Jesus has both 'Jewish' and 'Gentile' blood coursing through His veins. He has come to incorporate the Gentiles into the chosen family just like these four Gentile women had already been incorporated. God has always counted the 'spiritual seed' of Abraham as the true Israel (John 8:39). Because of Christmas (and Easter), everyone can be part of Jesus' family tree. This Christmas let us rejoice that we are "heirs of God and joint heirs with Christ" (Rom. 8:17). Christ wanted to be part of the human family to bring us into His family!

> "He came to His own, and His own did not receive Him. But as many as received Him, to them He gave the right to become children of God, to those who believe in His name: who were born, not of blood, nor of the will of the flesh, nor of the will of man, but of God." ~ John 1:11-13

December 13th
THE SON OF ABRAHAM
(MATTHEW 1:1; LUKE 3:38)

We observed in the last devotion that the opening line of the New Testament is about the lineage of *a son*. But not just any son. This is "the son of David, the son of Abraham" (Matt. 1:1).  While we focused on the significance of Jesus being "the son of David" yesterday, it is *just as important* to wrap our minds around why Matthew draws attention to Jesus being "the son of Abraham." For those whose minds have been steeped in the Old Testament the phrase "son of Abraham" will surely evoke the climactic event in Abraham's life—the Akedah. The binding and giving up of Abraham's "only son" in obedience to the Lord (Gen. 22).

Why should we hear an echo of this story? Because it is *the story* that brings into focus the prophetic promise that God's Son would one day become "the son of Abraham." To put it in broader terms, it is a story of Jesus becoming a son of Abraham so that Abraham's sons might become sons of God. Abraham knew, according to the customs of covenant cutting in his day, that if a covenant partner asked for your son that meant they were obligated to give you their son. And each son would grow up in the home of their father's covenant partner until they reached maturity. It was the ultimate sign of covenantal trust and loyalty between tribal chiefs. So when Abraham heard God say, "Take now your son, your only son Isaac, whom you love, and go to the land of Moriah, and offer him there as a ascension offering on one of the mountains of which I shall tell you" (Gen 22:2), he knew God was *covenantly bound* to give him His Son!

How do we know Abraham would have understood this covenantal arrangement? Well, Jesus said, "Your father Abraham rejoiced to see My day, and he saw it and was glad" (John 8:56). It appears Abraham *saw* God's gift of His Son, Jesus, because he understood the covenant process. As a covenant partner, God was not going to ask something from Abraham He in turn was not going to give. But there is one big difference. Abraham only *figuratively gave* his son as an ascension offering on a mountain in the land of Moriah. Once God saw Abraham's obedience, He mercifully stayed Abraham's hand (Gen. 22:12). But God *literally gave* His Son as an offering on a mountain in the land Moriah (2 Chr. 3:1). Jesus was obedient *unto death* (Phil. 2:8). When the Eternal Son of God *became a son of Abraham* in the womb of Mary, he enabled every son of Abraham to become sons of God! And who is a son of Abraham? The one who *believes* (Gal. 3:7).

During the Christmas season we celebrate God's faithfulness to His covenant with Abraham. We commemorate the Gospel truth that "God so loved the world that He gave His only begotten Son, that whoever believes in Him should not perish but have everlasting life" (John 3:16). Prophesying about this moment of eternal significance the prophet Isaiah declared, "A Son is given" (Isaiah 9:6). The Son of God *become Abraham's son*. A Gift surpassing all worth was dropped from Heaven. And this Gift is not simply for Abraham, this Gift is for *whoever believes.*

While we've focused on Jesus' genealogy in Matthew, *Luke's genealogy is also significant.* Matthew only goes back to Abraham, but Luke goes back further. His ends, "the son of Adam, the son of God" (Luke 3:38). The truth is, all humanity can trace their ancestry back to God, just as Jesus can. We are all "the son of Adam, the son of God" (Gen. 1:26; Acts 17:28). But our sonship in Adam has defaced the image of God in us and estranged us from God's family. We, like Adam, have lived east of Eden, east of God's domain and presence. Paul describes life outside of Christ like this—"alienated from God" and "by nature children of wrath" (Col. 1:23, Eph. 2:3). But God, in His great mercy, was not content to leave us that way!

At Christmas, a Faithful Adam would rise. And this 'Last Adam' wasn't simply a son of God by His descent from the 'First Adam'. No, He was also the Son of God in a totally unique way. He was the 'eternally begotten' Son. Jesus is part of the Primal Family that undergirds and upholds all time, space, and matter. He is not simply a son of God by creation like you and me, but the Eternal Son of God by nature. The Eternal Son, become the Son of Adam, become the Son of Abraham, given for you and me! If God gave us the greatest gift —Himself—surely we can offer ourselves to Him (Rom. 12:1).

"He who did not spare His own Son, but delivered Him up for us all, how shall He not with Him also freely give us all things?" ~ Romans 8:32

December 14th
JESUS' CIRCUMCISION
(LUKE 2:21)

Jesus was "born under the law, to redeem those who were under the law" (Gal. 4:4-5). The law stipulated that every male was to be circumcised "on the eighth day" (Lev. 12:3). This was something God began when He made a covenant with Abraham. God said, "He who is eight days old among you shall be circumcised" (Gen. 17:12). Thus, as a covenant child, born under the law, Jesus took the covenantal sign: "And when eight days were completed for the circumcision of the Child, His name was called Jesus, the name given by the angel before He was conceived in the womb" (Luke 2:21).

Jesus was so fully human that He endured the shedding of blood and removal of the flesh every eight day old Jewish boy endured. This foreshadowed when He would shed His blood for the *full removal of the flesh at the cross* so we could enter new life (Col. 2:11; Rom. 6:6). It is also very significant that circumcision happened on the eighth day. As we've seen, eight is the biblical number of new creation. It is no accident God appointed this day for the removal of the flesh as a sign pointing toward entrance into His promises and new creation life.

Unsurprisingly, it has been scientifically proven that the eighth day is *the perfect day* for circumcision. This was discovered in 1872 by Alexander Schmidt when he noticed how the level of prothrombin and vitamin-K spiked on this day allowing for sufficient blood clotting. Dr. Joseph Mercola says, "Day 8 is said to be the only time in a baby's life when his prothrombin level will naturally exceed 100 percent of normal." It is around 110%. While other ancient cultures practiced circumcision as a *puberty rite*, Israel was the only society that practiced *infant circumcision*.

God desired His covenant people to enter an 'anti-flesh pedagogy' the moment they came into the world. *It was meant to be a sign to the world (and them) that they trusted the promises of God rather than the corrupted powers of their flesh.* This is why Abraham was circumcised at 99 years old in Genesis 17. God wanted to show him that his and Sarah's 'fleshly strategy' of bringing God's promised seed through Hagar thirteen years earlier was all wrong. Abraham needed to stop trusting his flesh and instead trust in God who "who gives life to the dead and calls those things which do not exist as though they did" (Rom. 4:16-22). Sadly, the true meaning of circumcision would become corrupted by certain Jewish leaders around the time of Jesus and people began to make their boast in it! They made the sign of circumcision the exact opposite of what it signified!

God has always sought to remove the sinful side of our flesh (pride, bravado, violence, etc.). Circumcision was *a sign* of this removal. But the sign could not fully confer that which it signified. In Paul's language, it was part of the "weak and beggarly elements of the world" which God gave to His covenant community during a dispensation of "childhood" (Gal. 4:3, 9). It most certainly was "good and holy" *as a sign*, but to really get rid of the *sinful flesh* people needed "circumcised hearts"—they needed to get to the root of the sinful flesh and be made new *inwardly* (Rom. 2:29; 7:12; Deut. 10:16; Jer. 4:4). They needed "a circumcision not performed by human hands" where not just a little flesh was put to death but their entire being was "buried with him in baptism" (Col. 2:11-12). An inward circumcision where they become united with Christ and fully freed from indwelling sin.

Christmas reminds us that Jesus was born under the law. We are reminded that He lived in a way that fulfilled everything the law signified. While we are no longer bound by these 'child-training laws', the truth of what they signified should be "inscribed on our hearts" (Heb. 10:16). We still are called to "receive the witness" of the law (Rom. 3:21). And part of "the witness" of circumcision is that we must have "no confidence in the flesh" (Phil. 3:3). Christ lived in full reliance on the Father (John 5:19). He lived out circumcision's signification! We can rest in His work and see that work replicated in our lives. We can know and believe that when we are weak, then we are strong!

> "But he said to me, 'My grace is sufficient for you, for my power is made perfect in weakness.' Therefore I will boast all the more gladly about my weaknesses, so that Christ's power may rest on me. " ~ 2 Corinthians 12:9, NIV

December 15th

SIMEON THE SEER

(LUKE 2:25-35)

Forty days after Jesus' birth Mary and Joseph journeyed six miles from Bethlehem to Jerusalem (Luke 2:22). Mary would go through the "purification rites" the law required post-pregnancy and Jesus would be "presented to the Lord" as every firstborn Jewish male was (Ex. 13:2; Lev. 12:6-8). As the law permitted, Mary and Joseph gave "two turtledoves", instead of a lamb, because they were poor (Luke 2:24). Jesus wasn't born into a wealthy family in

Rome, Athens, Alexandria, or Jerusalem. Rather, He was the son of a lower-class family from Nazareth. The Creator of all things seen and unseen, and Owner of a cattle on a thousand hills, became *poor*. For *your* sake. Paul writes, "though He was rich, yet for your sakes He became poor, that you through His poverty might become rich" (2 Cor. 8:9).

While in the temple an elderly man named Simeon approached the holy family, took Jesus into his arms, and praised the Lord. He declared, "Sovereign Lord, as you have promised, you may now dismiss your servant in peace. For my eyes have seen your salvation, which you have prepared in the sight of all nations: a light for revelation to the Gentiles, and the glory of your people Israel" (Luke 2:29-32). Simeon's praise echoes the previous songs of Zechariah and the angelic host. The Lord has been abundantly faithful and has given a *Savior* not just for the Jews, but for the Gentiles as well. A Savior for all people!

The name Simeon means "to hear." Jesus would later say, "My sheep hear My voice" (John 10:27). Simeon exemplifies one *tuned to the Shepherd's voice*. Luke writes, "it had been revealed to him by the Holy Spirit that he would not see death before he had seen the Lord's Christ" (Luke 2:26). The ears and eyes of Simeon's heart were open and he was given a special revelation concerning the Lord's work in his own day. Not only that, but *Simeon was able to perceive when that word was being fulfilled in his midst.* His perception about what the Lord would do through Jesus caused Joseph and Mary to "marvel" (Luke 2:33). Do we have that impact on others when we speak about Christ? Are we so in tune to the *Light of the Gentiles* and the *Glory of Israel* that when we speak of Him people *marvel* and desire to hear more? Are our spiritual ears open to the Holy Spirit who takes what is Jesus' and discloses it to us? (John 16:14)

Simeon's story also fits well with the themes of Advent. He is an example of believers who are *waiting patiently* for the day when faith becomes sight. The day when they are caught up before the throne of the Lord and receive the promised *beatific vision.* John wrote, "But we know that when Christ appears, we shall be like him, for we shall see him as he is" (1 John 3:2). Paul said, "now we see in a mirror, dimly, but then face to face" (1 Cor. 13:12). In Revelation we are told, "They shall see His face, and His name shall be on their foreheads" (Rev. 22:4). This is *the blessed hope* of Christians. "And everyone who has this hope in Him purifies himself, just as He is pure" (1 John 3:3).

We are called to be like Simeon in the temple. Paul instructs us, "For the grace of God that brings salvation has appeared to all men, teaching us that, denying ungodliness and worldly lusts, we should live soberly, righteously, and godly in the present age, looking for the blessed hope and glorious appearing of our great God and Savior Jesus Christ, who gave Himself for us, that He might redeem us from every lawless deed and purify for Himself His own special people, zealous for good works" (Tit. 2:11-14).

Just as Simeon patiently waited "to see" the Messiah at His first advent, so we must patiently wait for His second advent. Just as Simeon was "just and devout" in his waiting, so we are to live "soberly, righteously, and godly in the present age." This Christmas let us be like Simeon. Let us hear what the Spirit is saying and patiently wait for the fulfillment of all of God's promises. As Simeon lifted Jesus in his arms, let us lift Jesus up for all to see and raise a hallelujah!

"We want each of you to show this same diligence to the very end, so that what you hope for may be fully realized. We do not want you to become lazy, but to imitate those who through faith and patience inherit what has been promised."
~ Hebrews 6:11-12, NIV

December 16th

ANNA THE PROPHETESS

(LUKE 2:36-38)

Anna experienced tragedy early on in life. Her
husband died only seven years into their marriage
likely leaving Anna as a widow in her early twenties
(Luke 2:36). Whether by choice, or undesired
circumstance, Anna would remain a widow the rest
of her life. If not right away, at some point Anna
seems to have accepted this lot in life and sought to
utilize her state to serve the Lord in a greater

capacity. We are told that "she never left the temple but worshipped day and night, fasting and praying" (Luke 2:38).

Many who have experienced tragedy, who have travelled through the valley of the shadow of death, have a strong appreciation of the importance and power of prayer. I think of David writing his powerful prayers while being chased and persecuted by Saul, or Elijah who called down fire amidst the persecutions of Jezebel, or Jeremiah who continued to pray and prophesy even though thrown down a well and left to die, or Daniel who was taken as a captive to Babylon and yet continued to pray regardless of what price he might pay. Like Anna these men knew "the prayer of a righteous man is powerful and effective" (James 5:16).

The fasting and prayers of a widow can truly shake nations! The early church understood the important role elderly widowed 'prayer warriors' had in the kingdom of God. They added certain respected widows, who were over sixty, to a list of those who would be provided for by the church. Paul wrote, "The widow who is really in need and left all alone puts her hope in God and continues night and day to pray and to ask God for help" (1 Tim. 5:5). In essence, Paul is saying that the sort of widows the church should be providing for are widows like Anna. Widows who are on the front lines of battle. Widows who are fearlessly brandishing the sword of the Spirit and interceding for the victorious march of the kingdom!

Anna is also said to have been "a prophet" (Luke 2:36). Upon seeing Jesus in the temple she "spoke about the child to all who were looking forward to the redemption of Jerusalem" (Luke 2:38). When someone is worshipping night and day near the Lord, like Anna, they can't help but begin to prophecy. To speak "edification and exhortation and comfort to men" (1 Cor. 14:3). To speak of the glories and unsearchable riches of the Messiah. And who are the people who hear? Those "who were looking forward to the redemption." Not everyone desires to hear the prophetic word about Jesus, *but some do.* There is always *someone* needing to hear what Christians have to say even if much of the world mocks us or is indifferent. Never fear the world. Instead fear that someone in your midst might never hear what you know they need to hear. Speak up! Be an Anna!

Anna was 84 years old when she met Jesus. That is seven times twelve. Seven is the biblical number of completion and twelve is the number of government. Her age is the number of perfected government. Some of the most foundational pillars in the church, in the government of God, are the grandmothers and elderly widows who pray. Anna is a beautiful picture of a widow who uses her singleness for service to the Lord. Singleness can be a great blessing. Paul writes, "An unmarried woman or virgin is concerned about the Lord's affairs: Her aim is to be devoted to the Lord in both body and spirit" (1 Cor. 7:34, NIV).

This Christmas let us be prayer warriors like Anna. Let us prophecy like there is someone who desperately needs to hear what we have to say. Let us not be overwhelmed about any tragedy that might have taken place in our lives, but rather see how God can utilize our situation in life for His glory. And just like Anna "gave thanks to the Lord" upon seeing baby Jesus, let us give thanks to the Lord for this greatest of gifts! Let us also frequent the House of the Lord—the collective gathering of the saints—like Anna. As we give our troubling circumstances over to Him and practice prayer and thanksgiving like Anna, it is all but certain bitterness, frustration, and hopelessness will never be able to take root in our lives!

"Devote yourselves to prayer, being watchful and thankful." ~ Colossians 4:2, NIV

December 17th

PRESENTING THE LAMB

(LUKE 2:22-24)

The reason Simeon and Anna encountered baby Jesus in the temple is because Mary was required to complete her "purification according to the law" and "present [her son] to the Lord" (Luke 2:22). First, Mary offered *two turtledoves* (Luke 2:24). Every Jewish woman would give a turtledove as a sin offering forty days after giving birth to a boy. Alongside of that, if a woman was poor she would give a second turtledove as an ascension offering. If she was not poor she would give a lamb (Lev. 12:8). Mary clearly is presented as *poor*. Second, a month after the first son of a non-Levite Jewish family was born he was to be redeemed from having to serve as priest. The price was "five silver shekels" (Num. 18:16).

While Luke records that the sacrifices for Mary's purification were given, he does not indicate that the redemption price was given. Instead of Jesus being "redeemed" Luke solely says He was "presented." Some scholars believe Jesus *was not* redeemed with silver. Why? Because He was not *simply* the first Jewish son in a family. At a deeper level He was the *spotless Lamb of God*. And when we look at the redemption passage in Numbers carefully we notice that "the firstling of a sheep" are not redeemed, instead their blood was to be "sprinkled on the altar" (Num. 18:17). Moreover, though Jesus was not a Levite, He was a priest. A priest "according to the order of Melchizedek" (Ps. 110:4; Heb. 5:6). Instead of being "redeemed", Jesus was "presented" in the temple as the *Perfect Priest and Sacrifice* who would redeem us by *sprinkling His own blood* on the altar (Heb. 9:12, 12:24).

Jesus was born to die. While this statement is at times mocked by those who desire to appear theologically sophisticated, it is *perfectly appropriate*. Those who make this statement are not saying Jesus was *solely* born to die, rather they are rightly bringing to light that His death was one of the *primary purposes* for His birth. Besides not being redeemed at the temple as a baby, how else do we know that? Because Jesus said so! In fact, it was the very thing He uttered as He entered our world! *Yes, the Bible actually tells us what the Word/Son of God was saying as He was becoming flesh for our salvation!*

"When He came into the world, He said: 'Sacrifice and offering You did not desire, but a body You have prepared for Me. In burnt offerings and sacrifices for sin You had no pleasure'" (Heb. 10:5-6). The Father desired the Body of Jesus. He desired the flesh and blood that would be born of Mary. The Seed of the woman. The book of Hebrews explains at length how the entire sacrificial system was simply "a shadow of the good things to come" (Heb. 10:1). God did not desire the sacrifices. He desired what the sacrifices pointed to. Only the *substance* of the *shadow* could deal with sin once and for all. In fact, "it is impossible for the blood of bulls and goats to take away sins" (Heb. 10:4). *The millions of slain bulls and goats simply pointed toward the Ultimate and True Sacrifice—the Body of Jesus.*

The Lord did not "take pleasure" in the slaughter and meticulous butchering process of the Levitical sacrifices. Yes, He commanded them. Yes, every element of each of the five Levitical sacrifices have spiritual signification. Nevertheless, the entirety of the system was simply a shadow, a faint representation, of how God ultimately desired to bring redemption. *Only the body of Jesus gave the Lord "pleasure."* The Body that came forth from Mary. The Body that lived in perfect obedience to the will of the Father. The Body that was beaten, scourged, and crucified for our salvation. The Body which *expired on the cross*, poured forth *water and blood*, was *wrapped in cloths*, and *laid in a grave for three days*. The Body which would not see corruption but rather resurrect to newness of life and ascend to the Father's right hand. This, and this alone, brought the Father pleasure!

Jesus was born to die. His death, and subsequent resurrection, was crucial to His mission of bringing about new humanity. As our hearts kneel before the Savior in the stable during the Christmas season let us remember that the stable was not simply filled with bleating lambs, but also with the soft whimpers of the Lamb who would make all things new. The Lamb who was not redeemed so that He could redeem you and me!

"In him we have redemption through his blood, the forgiveness of sins, in accordance with the riches of God's grace." ~ Ephesians 1:7, NIV

December 18th
KING HEROD
(MATTHEW 2:1-8, 16-18)

Jesus was born "in the days of Herod the king" (Matt. 2:1). About six months after Jesus' birth a caravan of magi came from the East to worship "the King of the Jews" (Matt. 2:2). These magi were not referring to King Herod. Rather, it was a king that had recently been  born, for they saw *the sign* of His birth in the sky. Matthew tells us, "When Herod the king heard this, he was troubled, and all Jerusalem with him" (Matt. 2:3). Why was Herod so disturbed by this news?

Herod was one of the more paranoid, power-hungry, and overall cruel kings from the ancient world. His sons from his ten wives were sort of like the sons from David's eight wives—*troubled*, to put it mildly. They vied with each other for power and eventually Herod would even imprison and execute some of them (along with one of his wives). Caesar Augustus once joked, "It is better to be Herod's pig than son." Pig and son sound similar in Greek so it was a pun, but more than that Herod did not eat pig (as a practicing Jew) so at least you would survive as Herod's pig!

Those who believe the Bible is the revelatory word of God should not be surprised that Herod was a power-hungry ruler obsessed with building projects as he sought to make his own name great. Over four hundred years before his reign the angel Gabriel had delivered a prophesy not simply about the coming of King Jesus (Dan. 7:20-27), but also about the wicked reign of Herod (Dan. 11:36-45). In one of my Bibles this section of Daniel has a heading titled "The King Who Exalts Himself." An apt title for Herod.

Gabriel said concerning this king, "he will honor a god of fortresses" (Dan. 11:38). His god would be *mammon* and *might*. Interestingly, Herod is known primarily for his building projects. He built the fortress Antonia, fortifications in Jerusalem and Jericho, and fortresses at Masada and various other cities. He also constructed several new cities, including Caesarea. One of his most renowned projects was a renovation of the temple in Jerusalem. The apostles said of these renovations, "Master, behold what manner of stones and what buildings are here" (Mark 13:1). But instead of seeking to bring glory to Yahweh through these building projects, he sought to glorify himself. In contrast, the true King of the Jews builds a temple that solely brings glory to God. King Jesus declared, "I will build My church, and the gates of Hades shall not prevail against it" (Matt. 16:18). Jesus was the *Greater Herod*. Herod in a sense was acting like an Anti-Christ. He was the 'false king' and 'false builder' of God's people.

The glory Herod sought for himself ultimately ended in shame. Gabriel said "reports from the east and the north will alarm him, and he will set out in a great rage to destroy and annihilate many" (Dan. 11:44). The "report from the north" likely refers to the news he heard about his son Antipater who was in Rome *conspiring to kill him* because his dad had killed his two older brothers. Upon hearing this news Herod killed Antipater as well! The "report from the east" likely refers to the report of the magi about the birth of "the King of the Jews." They came "from the East" (Matt. 2:1). In "great rage" Herod would massacre all of the children in Bethlehem "from two years old and under" (Matt. 2:16-18).

This Christmas let us thank the Father that the Everlasting King of the Jews has been born. This King is not power-hungry and cruel. Rather, He is a servant and kind (Matt. 20:28; Tit. 3:4). As citizens of heaven seated with King Jesus in heavenly places, let us join this Lord's "laughter" at those who plot against the reign of His Son like Herod did (Ps. 2). Let us "kiss the Son" knowing that He alone is King of kings and deserves our sole allegiance. Let us honor Jesus the Master Builder of God's temple and marvel at His great work instead of being like the disciples who marveled at Herod's work (Mark 13:1). Let us be assured that no wicked ruler, no Herod, not even that dragon of old (the devil himself), can prevail against Christ and His church (Matt. 16:18; Rev. 12, 20:10). Let us be comforted that Christ "weeps with those who weep" and will one day "wipe every tear" from the eyes of those who have been wronged by wicked rulers like Herod (Rom. 12:15; Rev. 21:4).

"Now to the King eternal, immortal, invisible, to God who alone is wise, be honor and glory forever and ever. Amen." ~ 1 Timothy 1:17

December 19th

O LITTLE TOWN OF BETHLEHEM

(MATTHEW 2:4-6)

"O little town of Bethlehem, how still we see thee lie..." Though mentioned throughout the infancy narratives, this little town is especially singled out in the story of the magi as having *immense prophetic significance*. The scribes and chief priests reported to Herod that the Messiah would be born "in Bethlehem of Judea, for thus it is written by the prophet: 'But you, Bethlehem, in the land of Judah, are not the least among the rulers of Judah; for out of you shall come a Ruler who will shepherd My people Israel'" (Matt. 2:5-6). Why did God choose this little town? What is the backstory of Bethlehem?

The first mention of Bethlehem is in Genesis. After giving birth to her second son *near Bethlehem*, Rachel dies (Gen. 35:19). Just before dying she named her son "Ben-Oni" which means "the son of sorrow." But his father renamed him "Ben-Jamin" which means "the son of the right hand" (Gen. 35:18). Jesus is the Greater Benjamin born in Bethlehem. He is first the "man of sorrows" who wept over Jerusalem, suffered, and died that we might have new life, but He has since been raised and seated at "the Father's right hand" to reign and intercede for us (Rom. 8:34).

We next think of Bethlehem in Scripture when it isn't named. The book of Joshua spends 43 verses naming 126 different towns and cities within Judah's inheritance. Bethlehem was so small and insignificant that it didn't warrant a mention! The scribes and chief priests who spoke with Herod quoted Micah's text about Bethlehem being "little among the thousands of Judah" (Mic. 5:2). Christmas reminds us that God loves to do monumental works in towns and villages that are seemingly insignificant and over-looked. We serve a God who especially loves the neglected parts of our world and proves it by having His Son born in this *little* town.

A third time Bethlehem comes into view in Scripture is when a Levite sinfully obtains a Bethlehemite concubine (Judg. 19:1). They are unfaithful to one another and their story ends in tragedy (Judg. 19:29). *Instead of a holy family in Bethlehem, we have an unholy family.* Thankfully, 1,200 years later a Faithful Priest would come from Bethlehem who would obtain a bride rather than a concubine. He would guard, love, and be faithful to her. He would reverse this tragedy.

Another mention of Bethlehem is in a famous story about two people who take a long journey there because it is where their family is from. There are men out in the fields, there is a nighttime redemptive scene, and there is the birth of a set-apart child. Know what story I'm referring to? No, not Mary and Joseph! This is the the story of Ruth and Naomi. These destitute women were provided for by a kinsman-redeemer from Bethlehem named Boaz (Ruth 1:2, 2:4). Ultimately, Jesus is the Greater Boaz. The Bethlehemite Kinsman-Redeemer who redeems a destitute and barren world.

The last time we read about Bethlehem in the Old Testament (besides Micah) is when Ruth's great-grandson comes on the scene—David. This young shepherd from Bethlehem would journey to a battlefield where all Israel was quaking in their boots before a giant serpentine enemy—a mighty Philistine wearing "scales" and inciting fear (1 Sam. 17:5). This Bethlehemite shepherd would slay this serpentine monster, crush his head, and become king (1 Sam. 17:51). It is the story of Jesus foreshadowed. The story of the Good Shepherd from Bethlehem who was manifested "that He might destroy the works of the devil" (1 John 3:8).

This Christmas let us be like the magi and be willing to journey to seemingly insignificant places like Bethlehem, and talk to seemingly insignificant people, because we know that God desires to be at work among the seemingly insignificant. And as we think of Little Bethlehem let us ponder the many glorious ways Christ fulfilled and gave deeper meaning to all the Old Testament stories of Bethlehem. Jesus always brings deeper meaning and fulfillment to every town and life He enters!

"God has chosen what is insignificant and despised in the world—what is viewed as nothing—to bring to nothing what is viewed as something."
~ 1 Corinthians 1:28, HCSB

December 20th

THE DANCING STAR

(MATTHEW 2:1-10)

"A star, a star, dancing through the night..." *Who is not filled with wonder at the thought of the star?* Matthew records four characteristics about this dancing star. First, it indicated the "birth of a Jewish king" (Matt. 2:2). Second, it "rose in the East" (Matt. 2:2). Third, there was an exact time it "appeared" and depending on the interpretation of the appearance it could have signaled the child was up to two years old (Matt. 2:7, 16). Fourth, after the magi arrived in Jerusalem the star "went before them to Bethlehem" and "stopped over where the young child was" (Matt. 2:9).

What was this star? There are two plausible explanations. The first is that it was a comet that lasted about 18-months like Hale-Bopp did in the 1990s. The other is that it was a 15-month journey of the planet Jupiter. I believe the 'Jupiter hypothesis' is *far more persuasive*. We actually have record of what Jupiter was doing in the night sky from 3-2 BC. We don't have any record of what would have to of been one of the most magnificent comets of that era.

So what would these Persian 'magi', these *professional star-gazers*, have seen? In September of 3BC, around Rosh Hashanah, Jupiter (the 'king wandering star') came into conjunction with Regulus (the 'king star'). While this happens every twelve years what made this conjunction unique was that Jupiter went into a double retrogressive 'dance' with Regulus (*a triple conjunction*)—something far more uncommon. Seeing the conjunction of these two 'king stars' occurred in Leo—*the lion constellation* (sign of Judah)—at the time of the Jewish New Year, one can see how these magi would interpret this as "king of the Jews."

And while Regulus and Jupiter were dancing at night in Leo, *during the day on Rosh Hashanah the path of the sun rose through Virgo (the 'virgin constellation') with a crescent moon at Virgo's feet.* This is what John saw in Revelation in the *apocalyptic nativity* of Revelation 12: "A great and wondrous sign appeared in heaven: a woman clothed with the sun, with the moon under her feet" (Rev. 12:1). The triple conjunction in Leo with the sun and moon in Virgo on Rosh Hashanah *was signifying the conception of "the Jewish King" in September of 3BC.*

Nine months later, Jupiter, the king planet (and second brightest planet) conjoined with Venus, the mother planet (and brightest planet) in such a close encounter that they created the brightest 'super star' in history. In fact, this event on June 17th of 2BC is shown in planetariums all around the world because of its unprecedented brightness. Having a super bright shining star in Nativity Scenes the night Jesus was born is actually very accurate according to the 'Jupiter hypothesis'. The star of Bethlehem was the brightest the *very night of Jesus' birth.* We will delve more into *when* and *how* the star "stopped" over Bethlehem in tomorrow's devotion.

This 'star' that led the magi was clearly not accidental. God is the one who ordered the heavens on Day 4. The sun, moon, and stars were for "signs and seasons" *on Earth* (Gen. 1:14). He also constructed the constellations. "He made the Bear, Orion, and the Pleiades" (Job 9:9). He brings out "Mazzaroth in its season" (Job 38:32). He perfectly crafted and ordered every star and "calls them all by name" (Is. 40:26). The magi knew they were not looking into a meaningless sky. They knew they weren't looking into a realm where stars randomly formed from molecular explosions. No, they were looking into the intricate craft and construction of an infinitely wise Creator!

God providentially planned for the constellations and 'wandering stars' to declare the birth of the Messiah in the fullness of time. He knew the exact time and place the Messiah would be born. We do not live on "an insignificant planet... tucked away in some forgotten corner of the universe" as an ill-informed famous astrophysicist once put it. Rather, we live in a *special position* in the universe with the stars and constellations *ordered around us* to "pour forth speech" (Ps. 19:1) We live in the place where God decided to become flesh for our salvation! (See Appendix A.)

This Christmas let us think about how God can use our lives to be a 'dancing star' to lead others to Christ. How can we paint a picture that Christ has been born?

> "Then you will shine among them like stars in the sky as you hold firmly to the word of life."
> ~ Philippians 2:15-16, NIV

December 21st

A GREATER HANUKKAH

(MATTHEW 2:1-12)

Did you know Hanukkah and Christmas have much in common? In fact, Hanukkah is much more biblical than many Christians think. It is prophesied about in Daniel and it is the setting of Jesus' lengthy Good Shepherd discourse in John (Dan. 11:21-35; John 10:22-23). Both Hanukkah and Christmas are winter festivals. Both have exchange of gifts. And most fascinating of all, if the 'Jupiter hypothesis' of the star of Bethlehem is correct, then both commemorate the dedication of the temple!

Hanukkah means "dedication." It is a festival that commemorates when the second temple, which had been desecrated for years by unfaithful priests and utilized for wicked pagan rituals under Antiochus IV, was recaptured by semi-faithful Jews and rededicated to the Lord. I say 'semi-faithful Jews' because while they made great strides in restoring proper worship they left out one crucial element—they did not inaugurate a priest from the line of Zadok as high priest. That was a grave sin!

In Daniel, while giving an in depth prophetic history from the time of Cyrus to Christ, Gabriel spoke about the reign of Antiochus IV. He calls him a "vile person" (Dan. 11:21). During his reign 40,000 Jews were killed and many sold into slavery. Though the Jews were in dire straights Gabriel prophesied that "they shall be aided with a little help" and "many would join this cause" (Dan. 11:34). This was a reference to the Jewish country boys known as the Maccabees. They would lead a band of fed up Jews to drive out the Greeks, recapture the temple, and "dedicate" it to the Lord over an eight day festival (the roots of Hanukkah).

While this revolt and rededication was a "little help", it was not the extensive help God's people really needed. Why? Largely because the Maccabean leaders themselves became corrupt. *Full help* and *full restoration* of God's House and people would not occur until Christ. What does all of this have to do with Christmas? Well, if the 'Jupiter Hypothesis' of the star is correct, the magi would have visited Jesus in the middle Hanukkah on December 25th, 2 BC! After seeing the super star in June, and traveling from Persia, the magi would have ended up in Jerusalem in November or December. Soon after their arrival Jupiter would have gone into its once a year retrograde. Meaning, it "stopped." From the vantage point of Jerusalem it would have "stopped" right over Bethlehem on December 25th!

What was significant about this day? Well, the first Hanukkah in 164 BC began on this day. Not only that, but in 2 BC the Hanukkah festival fell between December 22nd and 29th. The magi would have visited Jesus right in the middle of Hanukkah. On top of this, Christians celebrate Christmas with gift exchanges on December 25th. Strange coincidences? I think not! (For more see Appendix A.)

Jesus is the Greater Hanukkah. He is the Temple of God in the world (John 2:19). One reason there were eight day festivals at the dedication of Solomon's temple and at the rededication of the second temple during Hanukkah is because eight is the number of new creation. *Everything about the temple pointed to the promise of new creation.* Every aspect portrayed 're-entrance' into Eden. Well, it is only in Christ that we have a full re-entrance into Eden. With Him the veils are torn down, the walls of separation are bulldozed, and new creation life flows out of the temple to the entire world!

"The Word became flesh and tabernacled among us, and we beheld His glory" (John 1:14, my translation). This statement should be put in the mouth of the magi at every Christmas nativity program. The Greater Hanukkah was occurring and the Greater Temple was being lavished with gifts. The Shepherd of this Temple would not falter like the shepherds over the past two temples. He would be a 'everlasting help' rather than a 'little help'. He would be the Good Shepherd who would lay down His life for the sheep (John 10:11). Having been incorporated into the body of Christ, we too are "God's temple" (1 Cor. 3:16). Let us view Christmas as a time of Hanukkah. A time we can rededicate our own lives to the Lord.

> "I beseech you therefore, brethren, by the mercies of God, that you present your bodies a living sacrifice, holy, acceptable to God, which is your reasonable service." ~ Romans 12:1

December 22nd

THE MAGI'S GIFTS

(MATTHEW 2:11)

The magi did not come to King Jesus empty handed. They came *bearing gifts*. Matthew writes, "and when they had come into the house, they saw the young Child with Mary His mother, and fell down and worshiped Him. And when they had opened their treasures, they presented gifts to Him: gold, frankincense, and myrrh" (Matt. 2:11). These three gifts were all *very valuable*. Together they likely accounted for more wealth than Mary or Joseph were ever in possession of. More than enough to sustain them in Egypt while escaping *the deathly rage of Herod*.

The three gifts given to Jesus symbolize the primary offices He occupies. Jesus is king (gold), priest (incense), and prophet (myrrh). Jesus is what Adam was always meant to be. The *courageous kingly image-bearer* who takes dominion over the world. The *obedient priestly image-bearer* who leads His family in obedience to God's word. The *prophet* who after he has submitted to the Lord in all things (dying to self) has grown into a position of maturity where he is not simply a 'priestly servant' but also 'prophetic voice'—one who can discern between good and evil (1 Kings 3:9).

Besides symbolizing the offices of Christ, how do the magi's gifts tie into Hanukkah? At the height of the kingdom everything in Solomon's temple was overlaid with gold (1 Kings 6:21-22). Silver was "worthless" (1 Kings 10:21). At the first Hanukkah the Jews sought to restore that glory. They remade the gold furniture and "decorated the front of the temple with golden crowns and small shields" (1 Mac. 4:57, NRSV). 162 years later, when the magi arrive, they worship the One who would not just restore Solomon's glory, *but exceed it.* "A greater than Solomon is here" (Matt. 12:42). When the King is fully inaugurated at God's Right hand after His ascension, the 24 elders (likely angelic 'ancient ones') cast their golden crowns at His feet (Rev. 4:10). They recognize their rule over God's people has ended and it has now been granted to the "King of kings" and His human ambassadors (Rev. 19:16; Eph. 2:6; 2 Cor. 5:20). The magi *foreshadow* the full inauguration thirty-three years early.

What about frankincense? Incense was burned every morning and evening in the temple as a representation of the prayers of the saints (2 Chr. 13:11; Luke 1:10). An essential aspect of restoring the temple is restoring prayer. During Hanukkah "they offered incense on the altar" (1 Mac. 4:50, NRSV). They were remaking it into a house of prayer instead of a den for the pagan thieves. From the beginning the temple was envisioned as a house of prayer for the nations (1 Kings 8:41-43). By presenting Jesus with incense the magi recognized He is the House of Prayer for all nations and the Great High Priest who "always lives to make intercession" for us (Heb. 7:25). Our prayers are joined with His and *ascend like incense* into heaven. Because they ascend through our *Mediator* and *Great High Priest* they are so precious to God that they are gathered in *golden bowls* (Rev. 5:8).

How about myrrh? Psalms says the king's garments "are scented with myrrh and aloes" (Ps. 45:8). This was especially true after the King of the Jews was taken down from the cross and and wrapped in linen cloths with "a mixture of myrrh and aloes, about a hundred pounds" (John 19:39). The magi's gift of myrrh foretold this New Temple would be destroyed (John 2:19). But the Temple of Christ's body would not remain in rubble like Solomon's or Zerubbabel's did. This Temple would rise again in only three days. It never saw corruption and never will (Ps. 16:10).

Lastly, the gifts of the magi show us that Jesus—the New Temple—was dedicated with the wealth of the nations. The tabernacle was built with Egyptian wealth (Ex. 12:36). Solomon's Temple was built with the spoils of Israel's enemies (1 Chr. 18:11). Zerubbabel's temple was funded by Cyrus and built with Persian wealth (Ezra 1:6). The wealth of the nations has always been used to build the Lord's house (Prov. 13:22). This Christmas let us be like the magi and give monetary gifts which further Christ's kingdom. The Queen of Sheba came bearing gifts to Solomon but she ended up leaving with more than she gave (2 Chr. 9:9-12). No matter what we give to Jesus we must always remember that as the Greater Solomon He always gives more in return!

"And my God shall supply all your need according to His riches in glory by Christ Jesus."
~ Philippians 4:19

December 23rd

FLIGHT TO EGYPT

(MATTHEW 2:13-23)

The final episode in the Christmas narrative is more akin to a horror film than the dramas and sweet romances that preceded it. At this point King Herod was fully losing his cool. He was Herod the Hothead. He hated the very thought of a political rival and wanted to make sure the young Child the eminent magi had come to worship was no threat to his throne. So in maniacal rage "he sent forth and put to death all the male children who were in Bethlehem and in all its districts, from two years old and under" (Matt. 2:16).

This horrifying scene is referred to as 'the massacre of the innocents'. It shakes us awake and reminds us that the Christmas story is not simply sentimental. Christ fully entered *the real world*. He did not come to some fantasy realm where political leaders hold hands singing kumbaya. Rather, He was born in the midst of a war zone! He entered a world extremely hostile to Him and His Father. A world that was fully drowning in sin and massively in need of God's grace, redemption, reconciliation, and peace.

Though Herod would cause great pain for many Jewish households in Bethlehem, his ultimate scheme to murder Jesus was thwarted. Jesus was kept safe just like Moses had been during the massacre of the Hebrew infants in Egypt (Ex. 1:22, 2:3). The great deceiver, the devil, who was behind Herod's maniacal rage was himself "deceived" (Matt. 2:16). God gave both the magi and the holy family 'a way of escape' from Herod's rage. The truth is, *God always desires to deliver His people from evil* (Matt. 6:13; Mark 13:14). While the faith of the martyr is *noble* (Heb. 11:37-38), while their blood will be *avenged* (Rev. 6:11), God still regularly gives His people ways of escape so they can complete their assignments in this life. And that is what He did for the magi and Jesus!

How did the holy family escape? Well, dreaming Joseph had *another dream*. He was told in the dream, "Arise, take the young Child and His mother, flee to Egypt, and stay there until I bring you word" (Matt. 2:13). The magi had just been similarly "divinely warned in a dream" (Matt. 2:12). Upon awakening, Joseph became the protector he was called to be for his family and obeyed the divine word. He led his family with holy courage through a time of heated chaos. And Mary humbly complied with the heavenly word her husband received.

If the 'Jupiter hypothesis' timeframe is correct and the death of Herod was actually in 1BC, then the holy family was not likely in Egypt very long. More like *months* instead of the traditional view of *years*. But at the time of their obedience they had no idea how long their flight would end up being. They had to continue to trust the Lord every day on their journey. They had to continue to "ponder" everything they had been told by the angels, shepherds, and magi (Luke 2:19). They had to continue to say "amen" to their assignments like they had at the beginning (Luke

1:38). They had to "walk by faith and not by sight" (2 Cor. 5:7).

In due time God gave Jospeh two more dreams. An angel spoke to him in the first dream saying, "Arise, take the young Child and His mother, and go to the land of Israel, for those who sought the young Child's life are dead" (Matt. 2:20). A little later he was advised in a second dream to not settle in Judea because of Herod's son Archelaus. So he ventured north and settled again in his home town, Nazareth. Jesus would be raised as a Nazarene.

Joseph allowed the Lord to lead him every step of the way. There is a common thread of 'childlike trust' in the Christmas story. Those who followed the word of the Lord began to see wonders that astonished and amazed. Zechariah, Mary, Joseph, and the shepherds all heeded words from a member of the angelic heavenly host. The magi heeded the story of a member of the starry heavenly host. To the extent each character followed the light they were given, they were extraordinary blessed. This Christmas let us fearlessly and courageously trust the Lord's word above all else!

"Trust in the Lord with all your heart, and lean not on your own understanding. In all your ways acknowledge Him, and He shall direct your paths."
~ Proverbs 3:5-6

December 24th
THE CHILD GREW
(LUKE 2:39-52)

After returning to Nazareth Luke tells us, "the child grew and became strong, filled with wisdom. And the favor of God was upon him" (Luke 2:40, ESV). How often do we contemplate the growth of Jesus? The first time He smiled? When He first had strength to roll over? The first time He uttered 'abba' or 'ema'? The reaction on His face the first time He tasted mutton and bitter herbs? The joy of His parents once He mastered the Hebrew, Aramaic, and Greek alphabets?

For many, these thoughts are far too 'human' to attribute to Christ. Many Christians, intentionally or not, tend to think of a baby with a halo who immediately grows into one who can walk on water, multiply loaves, deliver perfect parables, and raise the dead. It seems unnatural to think of Christ growing physically and intellectually. But that is exactly what the Bible says happened. Jesus grew *body* and *soul*.

In fact, Luke mentions Jesus' growth in wisdom *twice*. After relating a story about how Jesus spent three days in the temple "astounding" the rabbis by His understanding and answers when He was twelve years old (Luke 2:46), Luke writes that Jesus *went back* to Nazareth and *again* "increased in wisdom and stature, and in favor with God and men" (Luke 2:52). While He "astonished" the religious leader's with His wisdom at a young age, by the time He reached thirty He would enrage them with *His otherworldly capacity to evade their verbal traps and trickery*. He was full grown at that point and *ready to enter His teaching ministry*.

Luke's statement about the growth of Christ echoes a statement about Samuel. In 1 Samuel we are told, "And the child Samuel grew in stature, and in favor both with the Lord and men" (1 Sam. 2:26). This should not surprise us. We have already seen that

Luke's infancy narrative echoes Samuel's infancy narrative. We've seen that Mary's magnificat is simply Hannah's song in higher key. (See December 5th.)

These two echoes of Samuel point toward Jesus being portrayed as a *Greater Samuel*. Jesus would replace the corrupt leadership in the Jerusalem Temple just like Samuel replaced the corrupt leadership of Eli's sons at the Tabernacle in Shiloh. Just as Samuel was a great circuit teacher who abounded in wisdom (1 Sam. 7:16), so Jesus is the *Greater Circuit Teacher* (Matt. 9:35) and *Fullness of Wisdom* (1 Cor. 1:30). Just as Samuel began the schools of the prophets, so Jesus gifted His Church with leaders so all Christians can be trained and grow in Him (Eph. 4:11-14).

Many different interpretative frameworks have been advanced by Christian scholars throughout the centuries to explain *how* Christ as *Eternal Wisdom incarnate* "increased in wisdom." While that discussion is not unimportant, I want to instead focus on how Christ can "grow" in His people. As members of His body we too are called to "grow", "become strong", and be "filled with wisdom."

After writing about how we have been "born again" from the "incorruptible seed of the Word of God", Peter says, "as newborn babes, desire the pure milk of

97

the word, that you may grow thereby, if indeed you have tasted that the Lord is gracious" (1 Pet. 2:2). We are called to *crave the Word* just as a baby *craves its mother's milk*. Why? *Because there is grace there.* Later Peter writes, "grow in the grace and knowledge of our Lord and Savior Jesus Christ" (2 Pet. 3:18). The *more* we drink, the *faster* we grow. Just as the baby ingests the mother's nutrients, so we ingest the *grace* and *knowledge* of Christ as we feast on His Word. We grow as we *feed*. We feed as we *read*. Eventually we are called to eat *meat* alongside *milk* (Heb. 5:12-6:1). To hunger after the "deep things of God" (1 Cor 2:9-10).

As we give gifts to one another this Christmas let us be reminded that Christ "gave gifts to men" (Eph. 4:8). He gave apostles, prophets, evangelists, pastors, and teachers so that we can "become mature, attaining to the whole measure of the fullness of Christ" (Eph. 4:13, NIV). Are you taking advantage of these gifts? Or are they neglected presents? Jesus didn't remain in the manger forever and neither should we. As we meditate on the growth of the human body and soul of Jesus, let us also contemplate our own growth in Him. And get to the place where we begin to "walk as He walked" (1 John 2:6).

"And do not be conformed to this world, but be transformed by the renewing of your mind, that you may prove what is that good and acceptable and perfect will of God." ~ Romans 12:2

December 25th

INDESCRIBABLE GIFT

(2 CORINTHIANS 9:15)

"Thanks be to God for His indescribable gift!" (2 Cor. 9:15) These words give voice to the gratitude and wonder we feel after having meditated on the infancy narratives. The only way we can do full justice to explaining the superabundant glory of Christmas is by confessing, like Paul, that the fullness of the Gift of Jesus is ultimately *indescribable*.

That the majestic gift of Jesus cannot be fully expressed by human language is communicated throughout Paul's letters. He describes "the riches of

Christ" as "boundless" (Eph. 3:8). "Boundless" can also be translated as *unfathomable, incalculable,* or *past finding out.* Paul uses this same Greek word to speak about the way in which God has brought salvation to the world. He writes that God's ways are "beyond tracing out" (Rom. 11:33). Ultimately, the "riches of Christ" gifted to us will be adored and appreciated *for all eternity,* and even then we will still not plumb their boundless depths (Eph. 2:7).

Paul prayed that those who have received the Gift of Jesus would come to "know" His love even though it "surpasses knowledge." He prayed that we would come to believe that God is able to do "exceedingly more" than we can "imagine" (Eph. 3:19-20, NIV). Human knowledge and imagination cannot contain the infinite riches of Jesus. We must mature to the place where we believe the Gift is far greater than anything we can conceive. His love *transcends knowledge.* His power exceeds the *wildest imagination.* This is one reason the Child is called "Wonderful" (Isa. 9:6). We are simply called to *be in awe* of the Child and *experience heavenly realities* like love, joy, and peace that "surpass understanding" (Phil. 4:7).

The fifth century church father, Augustine, gave a vivid illustration of what it means for the things of

God to be *indescribable*. Michael Pomazansky writes, "It is well known how Blessed Augustine, when he was walking along the seashore thinking about God, saw a boy sitting at the seaside scooping water from the sea with a seashell and pouring it into a pit in the sand. This scene inspired him to think of the disproportion between our shallow minds and the greatness of God. It is just as impossible for our mind to hold a conception of God in all His greatness, as it is impossible to scoop up the sea with a seashell."[3]

The Gift of Jesus, and the knowledge of God we obtain through Him, is so extensive that it cannot solely be appreciated with our intellect. It must also be experienced *with our heart*. The truth of who Jesus is must be meditated upon with a desire for the Spirit to *enlarge our understanding*. Mary knew this. When the shepherds came to her the night Jesus was born and shared what the Angel of the Lord and heavenly host declared, Mary "treasured up all these things and pondered them in her heart" (Luke 2:19, NIV). She had a lifetime to grow in understanding about how *wonderful* the Child on her bosom truly was. In fact, she has eternity to grow. If the mother of our Lord needed to "treasure" and "ponder" the *unsearchable riches* of Jesus, how much more you and me?

"Treasuring" the Gift of Jesus in our hearts should be our most important Christmas tradition. We should set apart time to ponder the infinite depths of His *person* and *work*. To appreciate the biblical *prophecy* and *typology*. To wonder at His *grace* and *new creation life*. To be in awe of the Charles Wesley lyrics, "Veiled in flesh the Godhead see. Hail the incarnate Deity." After meditating on the Nativity we should sing, "You are beautiful beyond description, too marvelous for words." Wonder should grip our hearts as we ponder the Infinite become finite for our eternal salvation!

This Christmas remember to unwrap the Gift of Jesus. He is the Seed of the Woman, the Lion of the Tribe of Judah, the Passover Lamb, the Great High Priest, the Prophet like unto Moses, the Kinsman Redeemer, the Bridegroom, the Rose of Sharon, the Prince of Peace, the Sun of Righteousness, the Giver of the Spirit, the Hidden Treasure, the Pearl of Great price, the Bread of Life, the Light of the world, the Good Shepherd, the True Vine, the Alpha and Omega, and much more! Who can fathom the depths of this infinite love? No one! But we can 'treasure' and 'ponder' these truths in our hearts.

"And there are also many other things that Jesus did, which if they were written one by one, I suppose that even the world itself could not contain the books that would be written. Amen." ~ John 21:25

December 26th

THE NICENE CREED: SANTA DEFENDS JESUS

The central claim of Christmas is that *God Almighty* took on flesh and was born for our salvation. The early creedal language of the New Testament put it like this, "Great is the mystery of godliness: God was manifested in the flesh" (1 Tim. 3:16). Elsewhere we are told that to see Jesus is to "see the Father" and that Jesus is "the image of the invisible God" (John 14:9; Col. 1:15). When considering where to place Christ in relation to the Creator/creature dividing line the church has always affirmed He is the on the side of Creator. He is the Eternal Son, the Word who spoke all things into existence, *made creature* for our salvation (John 1:1-14). There was never a time when the Son of God was not!

Our world was visited by none other than "I AM" (John 8:58). Jesus is not simply a heavenly messenger. He is not an angelic mediator at the top of the wrung of created spiritual beings. He is not like Hercules—a 'demigod' who has a human mother and heavenly father but was created in time with superhuman attributes. Rather, Jesus is truly and fully *God with us*. Immanuel (Matt. 1:23). As Paul put it, "In Him dwells the fullness of the godhead bodily" (Col. 2:9).

Preserving this central Gospel truth was the task of the first ecumenical council of the church. Convening a council of key church leaders to deliberate and decide upon doctrinal issues is not something foreign to Scripture. In fact, the apostles held a council with many important leaders in Acts 15 to deliberate on Jew/Gentile relations. Well, in the fourth century, twelve years after the conversion of the Roman emperor in AD 313, an invitation was sent out to the 1,800 bishops within the empire to come together in the city of Nicaea to deliberate another important theological issue. One deacon present at the council,

Athanasius, tells us that 318 bishops ended up gathering from all over the empire and even beyond. Athanasius' friend, the great theologian Gregory of Nazianzus, referred to the council as "the gathering of the three hundred and eighteen chosen men."

These 318 bishops were soldiers on the front line of a great battle. A prominent presbyter in Alexandria named Arius was teaching that "there was a time when the Son was not." Though Arius elevated Christ as 'the first of all creatures', and even found ways to affirm Him as 'the image of God', Arius still ultimately placed Christ on the side of *creature* rather than *Eternal Creator*. This was no small error and it was beginning to spread like cancer throughout the church. It needed to be dealt with decisively and with haste!

The 318 bishops cause us to think of the 318 servant-sons of Abraham who went to battle to rescue Lot (Gen. 14:14). The *chief servant* of Abraham was Eliezer (meaning "God has helped"). The gematria for Eliezer is 318. As Abraham's heir at the time, Eliezer went out as the head of Abraham's host in order to rescue family taken captive by the enemy. That is exactly what the 318 bishops at Nicea were doing. They were going to battle as God's heirs in order to *help rescue* those who had been taken captive by heresy and guard the truth about God's *eternally begotten* Son.

These bishops knew the pen is mightier than the sword. They crafted a creed as a bulwark against teachers of the persuasion of Arius who would try to infiltrate the church. A creed intent on protecting the truth of Christmas. In fact, nearly half of the creed deals with the truth of Christmas. (See Appendix B.) The truth of *who* the *person* of Christ is. Truths we will delve in deeper to in tomorrow's devotion.

One bishop from the city of Myra, Turkey was especially passionate about protecting the truth of Christmas. His name was Nicholas. Known today as St. Nicholas. Or, Santa Claus. Legend says that upon seeing Arius at the council St. Nick approached him and slapped him in the face! Though some scholars doubt the historicity of this story, Nicholas' bones show he died with a broken nose. He apparently was no stranger to standing up for truth! Santa knew the truth of Christmas was worth fighting for, even dying for. Imitating the tenacious faith of St. Nick, the young deacon Athanasius would end up being exiled for defending the truths of Nicea six times over the course of the next five decades! We turn to the truth he defended next.

"Now when Peter had come to Antioch, I withstood him to his face, because he was to be blamed."
~ Galatians 2:11

December 27th

ETERNALLY BEGOTTEN
OF THE FATHER
~ Athanasius The Great

The picture to the right is titled *Pantocrator*. Pantocrator is a Greek word that is used in the New Testament and simply means 'Almighty'. This particular picture is a very famous icon in Christian history dating back to the sixth century. It portrays Christ as the Almighty God clasping the New Testament in His left hand and pointing out to the world with His right hand as a sign of blessing. It is important to recognize that icons are *written* more than *drawn*. They are not attempting to capture what Jesus physically looks like as much as they are trying to *communicate theological truths* about

who He is. (Although, this icon does have striking resemblances to the Image of Edessa and Shroud of Turin.[4]) But the primary purpose of this icon is to communicate the theological truth that Jesus is *fully God* and *fully man*. This is why each side of His face is different. It is not poor *drawing*, rather it good *writing*.

The man most responsible for protecting the church against the 'Arians' who denied the full divinity of Jesus was Athanasius. Three years after attending the Council of Nicea as a deacon he was consecrated as bishop of one of the three most important cities in the Christian world at that time—Alexandria. He would serve as bishop for forty-six years (seventeen of those years being in exile while facing persecution from various Arian emperors). Being a man of short stature from Africa he was known as the 'black dwarf'. But though he was outwardly small, he emerged as one of the towering giants of the early church. For five decades he would be the primary apologist for the truth contained in the Nicene Creed. Christmas would not be the same today if God did not raise up Athanasius, and others like him, to defend His church from diabolical error.

The Creed states, "We believe...in one Lord Jesus Christ...the only-begotten, begotten of the Father before all ages... begotten, not made, of one essence with the Father." A lot of the debate surrounding the divinity of Jesus centered upon the biblical language of what it means for Jesus to be the "only begotten son" (John 3:16). The Creed sought to clarify this text by saying the Son was begotten "before all ages" and that being *begotten* is not synonymous with being *made*. Rather, it is a term about the *eternal relation* between the Father and Son instead of a term having to do with generation in time.

So, if 'begetting' does not have to do with *coming into existence*, then why was that particular term used in Scripture? Well, when something begets something else we understand that it begets "after its own kind" (Gen. 1:11, 21, 24). Apple trees beget *apple trees*, dogs beget *dogs*, apes beget *apes*, humans beget *humans*. So for the Son's relation to the Father to be one of 'begottenness' means that He is of the *same kind*, of the *same stuff*, as the Father. Whatever we say God the Father *is*, we can also say God the Son *is*. They are of the same order of species—Uncreated, Eternal, Invisible, Omnipotent, Omniscient, etc. Because God begets outside of time, in eternity, the 'only Son' is also eternal. God is *the eternally begetting One* (Father) and *the eternally begotten One* (Son). If God is eternally

'Father' then He must have always had a 'Son'. Duh! The Father *and* Son declared, "Let Us make man in Our image, according to Our likeness" (Gen. 1:26).

Athanasius understood these truths. He also understood the necessity of defending that Jesus was 'of one substance' with the Father (in Greek 'homoousia') because that was the word in the Creed the Arians despised the most. They despised it for two reasons. One, it is not used in Scripture. Two, it clearly defended the full divinity of Jesus. While it is one of the only words in the Creed not explicitly used in Scripture, Athanasius and the bishops who attended the Council understood it carried 'the sense of the Scripture'. It summarized the truth that dozens of Scriptures carry. So they decided to keep it in the Creed. The Arians wanted to alter the phrase with just one itty-bitty letter. The smallest Greek letter—iota. They wanted 'homoiousia' instead of 'homoousia'. But that smallest of letters changed the entire meaning of the word from 'same substance' to 'similar substance'. Athanasius' long career was largely a defense against the intrusion of this diabolical tiny iota. His career was an extended defense of the truth that "Immanuel" came and visited us at Christmas (Matt. 1:23). Not someone 'similar' to God, but God Himself! The leaders of the fourth century would not allow even 'one iota' to be added to the Creed. The Gospel and truth of Christmas literally depended on it!

"I and My Father are one." ~ John 10:30

110

December 28th

HYMNING THE MYSTERY
~ Ephrem The Syrian

Christmas carols have been part of the church from the beginning. One of the masters of song around the time the Nicene Creed was a Syrian deacon by the name of Ephrem. While men like Athanasius defended the truths of Christmas and Nicea with their theological treatises, Ephrem primarily defended it with hymns. Though only four hundred of his thousands of hymns are extant, thankfully a whole collection of hymns titled *Nativity Hymns* survives.

The power of song must never be underestimated. Martin Luther is said to have once remarked, "Let others write the catechisms and the theology, but let me write the hymns!"[5] Song captures people at the level of the heart. While many people do not read very much, most will listen to songs. And the songs that reverberate in our heart are the songs that set the tone for our life. Many Christians know of Luther's song 'A Mighty Fortress is Our God' while far fewer have read his short or long catechism. Many Christians know the classic Christmas Carols but few have ever read a Christmas devotional.

Ephrem understood the *power* and *importance* of song. In fact, one of the primary false teachers in Ephrem's town was promulgating their ideas through song and having great success. *Ironically, his name was Harmonius!* In order to combat his heresy Ephrem composed similar hymns, with similar meter, except free from Harmonius' poor theology. And, it worked! The people loved it! Many years later Luther would apply this same principle by taking tunes sung in the tavern and reworking them with Gospel lyrics. A way of 'plundering the wealth of the Egyptians' for the Lord!

While most English translations are outdated and have done a poor job capturing the beauty of

Ephrem's Syrian poetry, they are still worth reading. Why? *Because Ephrem was inspired to capture the deep theological truths of Christmas.* This is *unsurprising* seeing he served as deacon under a bishop who was one of the 318 who attended the council at Nicea. Like his bishop he desired to defend the truth of the full divinity of Jesus and be in service to the church.

In one nativity hymn Ephrem has Mary declare, "How shall I open the fountain of milk to Thee, O Fountain? Or how shall I give nourishment to Thee that nourishest all from Thy Table? How shall I bring to swaddling clothes One wrapped round with rays of glory?" And later, "The Babe that I carry carries me."[6] By singing these words one puts themselves in the place of Mary after she had fully pondered the truths of what it meant to be the mother of Immanuel. Truths that probably didn't fully hit her until after the resurrection and day of Pentecost.

Speaking of Mary, Ephrem sings, "The Lord entered her and became a servant; the Word entered her, and became silent within her; thunder entered her and his voice was still; the Shepherd of all entered her; he became a Lamb in her, and came forth bleating. ... Rich he went in, he came out poor: the High One went into her, he came out lowly. Brightness went into her and clothed himself, and came forth a despised form ... He that gives food to all went in, and knew hunger. He who gives drink to all went in, and knew thirst. Naked and bare came forth from her the Clother of all things."[7]

In another hymn Ephrem sings of the *abounding grace* that dawned on Christmas, "In this day of gladnesses let us not spread sadnesses! ... In this day when God came to sinners, let not the righteous be in his mind uplifted over sinner! ... On this day to us came forth the Gift, although we asked it not! Let us therefore bestow alms on them that cry and beg of us."[8]

Ephrem is only one of many great composers and musicians the Lord has raised up to lead the church in adoration of the Savior who was born in Bethlehem. May we have the 'awe' and 'wonder' that Ephrem had as he composed these hymns. May we sing with gusto the many great Christmas Carols the Spirit has inspired throughout the generations. And may we be inspired to write new and holy songs that will turn our own generation away from the Harmonius' of the world and toward truth!

"Be filled with the Spirit, speaking to one another in psalms and hymns and spiritual songs, singing and making melody in your heart to the Lord."
~ Ephesians 5:18-19

December 29th

HEARTS ABLAZE
~ Bernard of Clairvaux

Bernard of Clairvaux was an eleventh century Christian who is sometimes referred to as "the last of the church fathers." He has been loved and respected across denominational lines for his tremendous ability to communicate the love God has for us. One thing Bernard focused on in his Christmas sermons is how the message of Christ's birth should *set our hearts ablaze* and *fill us with inexpressible joy*. He wanted to make sure the message was not just seen historically, but was *personalized*.

In his Christmas sermons Bernard meditates on the phrase "Jesus Christ, the Son of God, is born in Bethlehem of Judea." He writes, "My soul has melted at these words. Yes, and my spirit burns within me as it hastens with its usual desire to communicate this joy and exultation to you. Jesus, Savior: what is so necessary to the lost, so desirable to the wretched, so useful to the hopeless? Where else would we find salvation?"[9] In another sermon he writes, "What heart so stony as not to be softened at these words? What soul is not melted at this voice of her Beloved? What announcement could be sweeter? ... O short word, telling of the Eternal Word abbreviated for us! O word full of heavenly delights! The heart is oppressed by its mellifluous sweetness, and longs to pour forth its redundant riches, but words refuse their service. So overpowering is the music of this short speech that it loses melody if one iota is changed."[10]

Bernard demonstrates that we are meant to respond to the message of Christmas like the angels. Heaven could not hold back the multitudes of the heavenly host as they swiftly flew to those fields of Bethlehem and thundered a joyous song about the Baby who had just been born. Their intellect was overflowing with wonder as they "desired to look into" the Good News of redemption through God's Son (1 Pet. 1:12). Our beings should be bursting with joy and filled with wonder just like the angels. We should be *absolutely overcome* by what took place the first Christmas Night!

Sadly, there are many people who have heard the message of Christmas, *but that message has yet to touch their hearts.* They are like the disciples walking from Jerusalem to Emmaus after Christ rose from the dead. Those two disciples had *heard* that Christ had risen, but they had yet to *believe* it. In fact, they were so unconvinced of the resurrection that instead of investigating the claim they left Jerusalem altogether! But Christ, in His great mercy, showed up to them in their unbelief. And He explained the resurrection in such a way from the Scriptures that their "hearts [began] to burn" and spring to life (Luke 24:13-35).

When Christmas is seen to be the story of the birth of a Savior *for you*, and you see it undeniably spelled out in God's Holy Word, your heart can begin to experience what Bernard's experienced. The Savior came to save *us* from *our* sin! (Matt. 1:21) In awe of this Savior Bernard wrote in another Christmas sermon, "One is coming who will cast all our sins into the depths of the sea, who will heal all our diseases, who will carry us on his own shoulders back to the source of our original worth. Great is the might, but more wonderful is the mercy in that the One who could help us willed to come to our assistance!"[11]

We must remember that "God did not send His Son into the world to condemn the world, but that the world through Him might be saved" (John 3:17). Jesus declared, "The Son of Man has come to seek and to save that which was lost" (Luke 19:10). Yes, if one rejects the coming of Jesus for them all that remains is condemnation (John 3:18, 36). But the coming itself is *not to be feared* but rather *embraced*. This is why Bernard writes in another Christmas sermon, "Do not flee, do not fear. He is not coming with weapons, he is seeking not to punish but to save."[12]

This Christmas rejoice that a 'Savior' has come to forgive you of all your sins! Rejoice that the Lord has given you a heart of flesh in place of a heart of stone. Allow your heart to be melted anew and burst with joy as you meditate on "'Jesus Christ, the Son of God, is born in Bethlehem of Judea." Personalize the Gift of Jesus. HE WAS BORN FOR YOU!

"Weren't our hearts ablaze within us while He was talking with us on the road and explaining the Scriptures to us?" ~ Luke 24:32, HCSB

December 30th

GOD COMES DOWN
~ Martin Luther

A great image for under-
standing what took place
at Christmas is an image
Jesus used for Himself in
John 1:51. He declared,
"Most assuredly, I say to
you, hereafter you shall
see heaven open, and the
angels of God ascending
and descending upon the
Son of Man." Jesus was
alluding to *Jacob's Ladder*

from Genesis. In that story Jacob was leaving the
Promised Land for fear of his brother's retaliation as
well as in order to find a wife from the family of his
uncle. And while leaving he was *met with a promise*. In a
dream he saw heaven opened, a ladder in between
heaven and earth, and "the angels of God ascending

and descending on it" (Gen. 28:12). From the top of the ladder the Lord thundered that He would fulfill the promises He made to Abraham and Isaac and be with Jacob until they were fulfilled (Gen. 28:14-15).

Jacob called the place of his vision Bethel, which means "house of God" (Gen. 28:19). The Lord graciously 'tabernacled' with Jacob in his midnight hour. When things were bleak, when Jacob likely had some level of fear or anxiety about his situation, that was *the exact moment* when God tore back the heavens, lowered a ladder, and shouted promises! Think about it, that is *exactly* what happened at Christmas. *Jesus is the Greater Jacob's Ladder. Jesus is the Gate of Heaven. Jesus is Bethel—the House of God. Jesus is the intersection of heaven and earth.* He is "the Temple", the One "come down from heaven", the "Door of the sheep", and "the Way" to Life (John 2:21; 6:38; 10:7; 14:6).

The movement of Christmas is *downward*. One thing Martin Luther emphasizes in his Christmas sermons is that Jesus came *all the way down*. In his words, Christ came "to the lowest depths."[13] By choosing Bethlehem over Jerusalem Christ chose "a dung heap."[14] Mary and Joseph were "the most insignificant and despised."[15] Luther says the work of shepherds is "low-down work, and the men who do it are regarded as trash."[16] Christ was so despised by the world around him that Mary "had to go to a cow stall and there bring forth the Maker of all creatures because nobody would give way."[17] After reminding us that only a few shepherds visited Jesus on this most holy of nights, Luther says, "when a cow calves more people know about it than have heard of this king."[18]

Luther does his best to look at every detail in the Christmas story that hints at a lowly and despised birth among lowly and despised people. Why? Because that is a great comfort to *us*—the lowly and despised! Christ came as the "least of these" so we could recognize Him in the "least of these." Christ came as a baby so we would draw near Him rather than draw back like the Israelites at Sinai. Luther writes, "To me there is no greater consolation given to mankind than this, that Christ became man, a child, a babe, playing in the lap and at the breasts of his most gracious mother. Who is there whom this sight would not comfort? Now is overcome the power of sin, death, hell, conscience, and guilt, if you come to judge this gurgling Babe and believe that he is come, not to judge you, but to save."[19]

In the middle of the night, heaven opened. And the Lord of glory did not just thunder promises from the top of a ladder in heaven, rather, He climbed all the way down the ladder and *fulfilled His promises*. The missionary E. Stanley Jones wrote, "All other faiths are philosophies or moralisms – man's search upward. The Gospel is God's search downward. Religions are man's search for God; the Gospel is God's search for man. There are many religions, but one Gospel."[20]

Christmas is Gospel. It is "good news" of "great joy" for "all people" (Luke 2:10). Let us come boldly to the manger because Christ has come mildly to us. The King is our brother, of our same flesh and blood, who is for us and not against us (Heb. 2:14; Rom. 8:31). We are among those who "trust God who justifies the ungodly" because "Christ died for the ungodly" (Rom. 4:5; 5:6). Christ chose the foolish, the weak, the base, and the despised (1 Cor. 1:26-31). David reminds us, "You stoop down to make me great" (2 Sam. 22:36). Never forget that God came to the lowest depths at Christmas!

"Who is like the Lord our God, the One who sits enthroned on high, who stoops down to look on the heavens and the earth? He raises the poor from the dust and lifts the needy from the ash heap; he seats them with princes, with the princes of his people."
~ Psalm 113:5-8, NIV

December 31st

BE BORN IN US TODAY
~ Phillips Brooks

The picture to the right is an artistic rendition of a famous Pharisee Jesus met one night in Jerusalem—a man named *Nicodemus*. He was a powerful man within Judaism. He was part of the top ruling council in the city of Jerusalem called the Sanhedrin. He  would have been a *highly respected* teacher by many pious Jews throughout Israel. And yet, for all his learning, and all his prestige, he did not understand one of the *basic principles* of the kingdom of God that Jesus was bringing. And that was this: "You must be born again" (John 3:3, 7).

Jesus went on to explain to Nicodemus that the 'second birth' he needed was a spiritual birth. He said, "That which is born of flesh is flesh and that which is born of Spirit is spirit" (John 3:6). Jesus was saying that something needs to happen *on the inside* of our lives if we are to enter the kingdom of God. He is basically hinting at the truth Paul lays out that we are "dead in trespasses and sins" and are in need of regeneration by the Spirit (Eph. 2:1; Tit. 3:5). That what is needed is not reform of the old man, but rather the "putting off of the old man" and the "putting on of a new man" (Col. 3:9-10). What is needed is *nothing less than* "new creation" (2 Cor. 5:17).

When Nicodemus first came to Jesus he said, "Rabbi, we know that You are a teacher come from God; for no one can do these signs that You do unless God is with him" (John 3:2). There are many people in the world like Nicodemus who marvel at the great works of God. They might even think Christmas is pretty neat. *But these people also are afraid of getting too close to Jesus,* especially publicly. (That is why Nicodemus came to Jesus at night.) The cost to one's reputation or subsequent life changes just seems too great to actually publicly 'come out' and *embrace* Jesus.

But simply being a *fan* of Jesus, simply being someone who enjoys the Christmas season, is not enough. One must become a *follower* of Jesus. And in order to truly become a *follower* of Jesus, one must have a *second birth.*

One must place their faith in Him. One must come to not simply marvel that He was born of Mary, but believe that He can be born *in them*.

The Christmas Carol 'O Little Town of Bethlehem' basically ends with this invitation. The last verse says, "O holy Child of Bethlehem, descend to us, we pray, cast out our sin and enter in, be born in us today."[21] These words were penned by a man named Phillips Brooks. A Harvard educated Episcopalian priest who has been called "the greatest American preacher of the 19th century." He was of the *Nicodemus class*. But, he understood the *necessity* of having a personal faith! He understood the importance of being born again! He understood that being a Christian is not simply about being a *fan*, it is about being a *follower*. It is about *experiencing new birth*. He penned these words after assisting a Christmas Eve service in Bethlehem in 1865 at the traditional site of Jesus' birth. He knew what happened *there* two millennia ago needed to happen *everywhere*.

Maybe Brooks was influenced by great preachers like Bernard or Luther who also emphasized *appropriating Christ personally*. Bernard said, "If only we too may be found a Bethlehem of Judah, that he may deign to be born within us too."[22] Luther said, "Of what benefit would it be to me if Christ had been born a thousand times, and it would daily be sung into my ears in a most lovely manner, if I were never to hear that he was born for me and was to be my very own?"[23]

The Good News of Christmas is that a Savior has been born. That is objective reality. No one can change the glorious reality of salvation available for all people. But, do you know the Savior been born 'for you'? Has the Savior been born 'in you'? Has the Spirit of God come into your life and made you new? This is the end goal of Christmas. That Christ in Bethlehem would be the first of many holy births. Say this prayer, "Lord Jesus, I don't simply want to be a 'fan' like Nicodemus, I want to be a 'follower'. I am a great sinner, but you are a Great Savior. I ask you to come into my heart right now. I want to be Your manger. I want to be Your home. Now and forever. Amen."

"But when the kindness and love of God our Savior appeared, he saved us, not because of righteous things we had done, but because of his mercy. He saved us through the washing of rebirth and renewal by the Holy Spirit, whom he poured out on us generously through Jesus Christ our Savior, so that, having been justified by his grace, we might become heirs having the hope of eternal life."
~ Titus 3:4-7, NIV

Appendix A

The Date of Christ's Birth

The purpose of this appendix is to give a longer defense of the 'Jupiter Hypothesis' for the Star of Bethlehem that was briefly discussed in the devotions *The Dancing Star* and *A Greater Hanukkah*. According to this hypothesis the star the magi observed was the movement of the *wandering star* Jupiter in 3-2 BC. For a popular defense of this position one can watch the 2007 documentary "The Star of Bethlehem" by Rick Larson and visit his website bethlehemstar.com. (See this end note[24] for some deficiencies in Larson's work.) Those interested in a more in depth read can pick up the 1991 book *The Star That Astonished The World* by Ernest Martin. For a shorter read, AS Haley has written a wonderful blog series on the subject under the name Anglican Curmudgeon.[25] These men, alongside many other astronomers and theologians, make *very compelling* cases that the star the magi followed was the 15-month journey of Jupiter through the night sky.

So, who were the magi? Why were they convinced the starry sky declared a king of the Jews had been born? The only detail Scripture gives us is that they were "from the East" (Matt. 2:1). Most likely *Persian magi*. And according to Scripture we know that at the high point of Babylonian/ Persian rule Daniel was placed as "chief over all the wise men of Babylon" and "chief of the magicians" (Dan. 2:48, 4:9). As a true prophet of God Daniel would have led these highly educated star gazers in the art of *true interpretation* of the night skies. It is likely that a group of truly converted 'god fearing' magi persisted in the 'school of Daniel' all the way through the Babylonian and Persian courts until the time of Christ. Some scholars note a passage by the Jewish philosopher Philo (a contemporary of Christ) which speaks about a group of Persian magi in his day who were "acquainted with the truth" and "initiate others in the divine virtues by very clear explanations."[26] (More on what the 'school of Daniel' might have looked like later.)

This explanation of a god-fearing group of Persian magi who had a purified understanding of God's handiwork in the heavens makes a lot of sense. Why would one come to "worship" a poor peasant baby who you believed to be "the king of the Jews" unless you were *already a believer* in the God of the Jews? These magi likely were not simply interpreting the heavens with purified understanding, but they would also have been aware of Daniel's great prophecy of "seventy weeks" of years that was coming to an end (Dan. 9:24). An unprecedented heavenly sign around the same time a heavenly prophetic timeline was running out was the perfect storm to cause many of these devoted men to make the *one thousand mile journey from Persia* to the little town of Bethlehem.

So, what exactly did the magi see in the night sky? Well, through the use of computer software we can observe exactly what the skies looked like anywhere in the world. The 'Jupiter Hypothesis' utilizes this software and looks at the night sky from the vantage point of Babylon. It shows how the planet Jupiter journeyed through a whole course of significant movements over the span of 15 months with *three stand-out signs*. The *first stand-out sign* occurred on September 3rd of 3 BC. That day happened to be *Rosh Hashanah*—the Jewish New Year. Before and after that date, over the course of a few weeks, the king planet (Jupiter) had a triple conjunction with the king star (Regulus) in the constellation of Leo (Lion). While this 'kingly dance' was happening at night in Leo, in the day time on September 3rd the path of the sun rose through Virgo (Virgin), with a crescent moon at

Virgo's feet. This is what John saw in the *apocalyptic nativity* of Revelation 12. The hypothesis is that this was *the day* when one of the heavenly host, Gabriel, announced that the virgin would give birth to the king of the Jews. God was telling the same story in the starry heavenly host as he was in Mary's home with a member of the host of the highest heavens.

Nine months later *the second stand-out sign occurred*. In June there was a triple 'super conjunction' between Jupiter (king planet) and Venus (mother planet). The closest conjunction occurred as the sun set on June 17, 2 BC. The two planets joined in such a way to give off light in the night sky like never before. AS Haley writes of this conjunction, "Venus as an evening star has apparent magnitude of -4.3 (the brightest nonlunar object in the night sky), while Jupiter's apparent magnitude is around -1.8, their combined apparent magnitude of greater than -6 would have been far brighter than any other object ever seen in the night sky other than the moon itself (which even in its full phase is about magnitude -12)."[27] This was 286 days after the first sign. Pregnancy lasts on average 280 days. So if Jesus was conceived the day of the annunciation He would have been born about six days later than the average child, but well within normal pregnancy bounds.

Many adherents of the 'Jupiter Hypothesis' claim this sign would have triggered the magi to *set out to Jerusalem from Persia*. They had seen two very rare triple conjunctions symbolizing the birth of a Jewish King and witnessed the brightest star in history. Ezra took four months to make the journey from Babylon to Jerusalem (Ezra 7:9). We can imagine after all their preparations and planning the magi took around the same time, *but likely a little longer*. This would put them in Jerusalem around November or December. Well, on December 25th of 2 B the *third stand-out took place*. Jupiter began to go into *retrograde motion*. From the human perspective that meant it "stopped" in the sky for six days.

Matthew writes, "When they heard the king, they departed; and behold, the star which they had seen in the East went before them, till it came and stood over where the young Child was" (Matt. 2:9). The magi were given two witnesses. They had the witness of Holy Scripture which the scribes in Jerusalem quoted saying the Christ would be born in Bethlehem, and they had a second witness in that the star they were following "stopped" *directly over* the place the scribes just told them the Christ would be born! Astronomer Ernest Martin writes, "In 2 BC as viewed from Jerusalem, Jupiter came to its normal stationary position directly over Bethlehem on December 25th."[28] If you drew a straight line from where Jupiter "stopped" down to the ground that was right where Jesus was living in Bethlehem! The magi followed that star, entered Bethlehem, and likely after some short conversations found "the house" where "the child" was (Matt. 2:11).

This is the basics of the 'Jupiter Hypothesis' as expounded by Martin, Larson, and others. While Martin brings up the connection to Hanukkah, Larson does not. For instance, Martin writes, "It happened to be the precise time for their feast of Hanukkah... the Feast of Dedication... They looked on Hanukkah as a second feast of Tabernacles which symbolized the redemption of the Jews and the entire world to God.... This was the traditional time for 'gift-giving.'"[29] Having originally been exposed to the 'Jupiter Hypothesis' through Larson, I did not initially know of the scholars who have made the connection to Hanukah. In fact, when I wrote the devotion *A Greater Hanukah*, I was not aware of any such scholars. I was certain someone must have drawn these conclusions, but I had not found them yet. So, how did I arrive at my own Hanukkah conclusion? Well, in 2019

Hanukkah and Christmas overlapped. Hanukkah fell between December 22-30. Because I was immersing myself again in the 'Jupiter Hypothesis' I began to wonder whether December 25th of 2 BC (the day Jupiter "stopped" over Bethlehem and the magi presented Christ their gifts) also coincided with Hanukkah. After looking at some Jewish calendars and performing a few semi-simple mathematical computations I discovered that not only did the magi come to visit Jesus during *the middle of Hanukkah*, but *the very first Hanukkah* under the Maccabees fell on December 25th as well! Because Sunday of 2019 fell on December 22nd (the first day of Hanukkah for both 2019 and 2 BC) I decided to preach a Christmas sermon titled "Jesus the Greater Hanukkah." I excitedly shouted the truths of the star of Bethlehem and Jesus as the True Temple to my congregation. A year later the short devotion in this book was written off the basic structure of that sermon.

Over the course of 2020 and 2021 I ended up running across some scholars and theologians (like Ernest Martin) who also made the connections between our modern day Christmas and Hanukkah. For instance, while doing a Bible Study on the Gospels in 2020 I ran across this statement by Peter Leithart, "On December 25, 164 they consecrated the altar in Jerusalem and began the sacrifices—this is the origin of the feast of Hanukkah. It is a restoration of pure worship."[30] It was reassuring to see that one of my favorite theologians had arrived at the same date I had. Concerning Hanukkah at the time of Jesus' birth, I was recently encouraged to see that Wierwille wrote in a 1982 book about the magi, "their journey brought them to Jerusalem in December, at which time a joyous festival called the Feast of Dedication, Hanukkah, took place... the Magi were coming to pay respect to, or worship, the young King of the Judeans, who was the true Temple."[31] Though references to this are far and few in between (in my limited research), they exist.

131

Hopefully more pastors and theologians begin to see the wondrous connections between the birth of Christ and the Feast of Dedication/Hanukkah. Hopefully this can become a tool of evangelism to the physical seed of Abraham!

Now back to the 'Jupiter Hypothesis'. The major hurdle that needs to be overcome for scholars to accept this hypothesis is the date of Herod's death. The fact is, the *majority of scholars* for the last four hundred years have dated Herod's death to 4 BC, rather than 1 BC. This date has been especially entrenched since the publication of Emil Schürer's classic text *The History of the Jewish People in the Time of Jesus Christ* in 1874. Many see Schürer's arguments as making an airtight case for the 'early date' of Herod's death. Even before Schürer bolstered the early date, Kepler and other astronomers of the 17th century only looked for the Bethlehem star from the year 5 BC and earlier because they were convinced that Herod died in 4 BC as well. Because of this, Kepler never saw the glorious story the 'wandering star' Jupiter told from 3-2 BC. That story had to wait to be told by more recent astronomers/theologians who were not bound to the 4 BC date for Herod's death and were able to have a more expanded time frame to investigate the ancient night skies.

Frustratingly, students of biblical history are bound to run across information about the date of Herod's death as if it is *established fact*. In light of that, I want to give a short defense of the late date for Herod's death. The *primary reason* I accept the late date for Herod's death is because I believe it is the most faithful to Scripture's own chronology. (Larson's film suffers a little on this front. He does not deal with the biblical chronology and throws people confidence solely on the veracity of his claims about a scribal error.) I do not accept the late date because I think the 'Jupiter Hypothesis' is awesome (though it is), but I accept it on the basis of the authority of Scripture. After the *primacy of Scripture's own chronology* for Herod's death is investigated we can *secondarily* investigate claims from other sources like Josephus.

What is the chronology Scripture gives? Well, *the Bible gives two key chronological markers to help us arrive at the date of the birth of Jesus (and thus the appearance of the star and death of Herod).* The most important marker is one Luke gives in the third chapter of his Gospel. He writes, "Now in the fifteenth year of the reign of Tiberius Caesar... the word of God came to John the son of Zechariah in the wilderness... Now Jesus Himself began His ministry at about thirty years of age" (Luke 3:1-2, 23). Without controversy historical records assure us that Tiberius Caesar succeeded Augustus Caesar on August 19th, AD 14. Thus the beginning of John's ministry fifteen years later would have been AD 29. We know Jesus began His ministry after John. Likely, six months after. *This would place the beginning of Jesus' ministry in late AD 29 or early AD 30.*

How then could Jesus be born in 8-5 BC like many modern scholars assure us? That would mean Jesus was anywhere from 34 to 38 years old when He began His ministry. The answer is simple. Many liberal scholars will just claim that Luke got his dates wrong. Whereas conservative scholars who believe in the reliability/truthfulness of Scripture tend to argue that Tiberius Caesar began to govern the provinces jointly with Augustus in 12 BC and that Luke was dating his "reign" from that year instead of from the day his actual reign began. But even that date doesn't push things early enough for Jesus to begin His ministry at thirty and be born from 8-5 BC. Using Occam's razor the simplest resolution, of course, is that Jesus was born in 2 BC, there was no year zero, and He truly did begin His ministry at the age of thirty in the actual fifteenth year of the reign of Tiberius Caesar around late AD 29 or early AD 30.

The second chronological date is from the infancy narrative. Luke writes, "And it came to pass in those days that a decree went out from Caesar Augustus that all the world should be registered. This census first took place while Quirinius was governing Syria" (Luke 2:1-2). Unlike the reign of Tiberius Caesar which we have a very clear date for, there is some dispute about the date of this decree because we don't know with *absolute certainty* which decree it is referring to. But the most reasonable answer, which is highly probably compared to all other suggestions, is that this decree refers to the silver jubilee of the rule of Augustus which coincided with the 750th anniversary of Rome in the year 2 BC. During this year Rome had many great celebrations for Augustus and the Senate conferred the title of *Pater Patriae* on him ('Father of my Country'). A special census was taken where the inhabitants of Roman rule where called to swear allegiance to Caesar. The early fifth century church historian, Orosius, wrote, "This is the earliest and most famous public acknowledgment which marked Caesar as the first of all men and the Romans as lords of the world."[32] *Ironically, the true lord of the world, Jesus, was coming into the world as Caesar was making this pretentious claim!* Many early church theologians and historians who date Christ's birth to 2 BC "declared that it was possible to verify the 'census' in official Roman records... and Tertullian (A.D. c. 145-220) mentions the records of the census 'kept in the archives of Rome.'"[33] Josephus also mentioned that at this time "all the people of the Jews gave assurance of their good will to Caesar."[34]

Accepting the 2 BC 'Jupiter Hypothesis' date for Jesus' birth not only fits with the biblical chronological markers of the reign of Tiberius and decree of Caesar Augustus, but it also fits perfectly with one of the two possible dates for Jesus' crucifixion. According to all four Gospels the death of Jesus happened just hours before the Sabbath at the time of the Passover. *This leaves only two possible dates for Christ's crucifixion.*

Friday April 7, AD 30 or Friday April 3, AD 33. The number of Passovers in the Gospel of John hint that Jesus' ministry was three and half years long and that has been the almost unanimous testimony of the church through the centuries. Three and a half years also fits *perfectly* with Daniel's prophecy that the Messiah would "be cut off" in the "the middle" of the last week of years when He would bring an end to sacrifice (Dan. 9:27). So the April 3, AD 33 date *fits perfectly* with Jesus' ministry beginning in late AD 29 or early AD 30 at the age of thirty.

So if Scripture's own chronological markers seem to be fairly straightforward that the birth of Christ could not be earlier than 2 BC, why do so many scholars today believe that Herod died in 4 BC and that Jesus's birth was in 5 BC or before? The primary reason for their position is that 4 BC *appears* to be the date given by the Jewish historian Josephus. He *apparently* says Herod captured Jerusalem in 37 BC and reigned for 34 years after that. Even if those are the original numbers Josephus actually gave, there is no reason to believe Josephus numbered Herod's reign inclusively or using non-accession reckoning. So one could just as easily put his death at 3 BC instead of 4 BC going by those dates. But most scholars choose 4 BC because that is the date Josephus' sons are said to have entered their reigns and a prominent lunar eclipse occurred on March 13, 4BC which they argue is the eclipse Josephus refers to happening right before Herod died. So 4 BC is strongly pushed.

Seeing the dates Josephus *appears* to give don't naturally fit the biblical chronology, how reliable is he? Should the dates he assigns to events always be trusted? Well, while they have largely been trusted by modern academia, about one hundred years ago a French historian, archaeologist and jurist named Theodore Reinarch began to put more scrutiny on many errors in Josephus' writings. Throughout his translation of Josephus he intersperses comments like "in another book his figures are different" or "this is a mistake." For instance, Reinarch highlights the fact that Josephus gives *three contradictory dates* for how long Hyrcanus reigned, *two separate dates* for arriving at when Herod died (8-7 BC or 4-3 BC), and *two separate dates* as to when Aristobulus set the diadem on his head. In light of Josephus' self-contradictory scholarship when it comes to giving exact dates for historical events, especially for monarchs, the date(s) he gives for Herod should *at the very least* be viewed with caution.

So, why the dogmatism in academia about the 4 BC date? Well, even if Josephus is wrong about the date of Herod's death, one additional hurdle is that 4 BC seems to fit with the beginning of Herod's sons reigns. While others have pointed out why this is not a problem in the past, one of the best treatments of this subject is a very recent article by Andrew E. Steinmann and Rodger C. Young. Summarizing their findings in their article "Evidences That Herod the Great's Sons Antedated Their Reigns to a Time before Herod's Death" they write, "We note that ancient historians, notably Josephus, contain indications that Herod's sons received royal prerogatives before Herod's death. It is proposed that this happened sometime in the year that began in Tishri 6 BC, and it was to this date that Herod's sons back-dated their reigns which actually began sometime in 1 BC. We also examine the numismatic evidence of the coins issued by Herod and his sons and demonstrate that it confirms this view, thereby removing the final pillar that supports the consensus chronology for Herod's reign."[35] I find their arguments thoroughly convincing.

Another problematic aspect of relying on Josephus for the date of Herod's death is the existence of multiple contradicting manuscripts. While 4 BC was being defended in most of academia since the 1500s, in 1629 the scholar

Joseph Justus Scaliger quoted a manuscript of Josephus that said Philip the Tetrarch died in the twenty-second year of Tiberius's reign instead of the twentieth year. That would bring Herod's death from 4/3 BC to 1 BC, which is the date Scaliger defended regarding the birth of Christ. About three centuries later W. E. Filmer followed in his footsteps and wrote a very important article in the *Journal of Theological Studies*. He says, "F. Riess quotes the Franciscan Molkenbuhr as saying that he had seen early copies of Josephus, one a Parisian copy dated 1517 and another a Venetian copy dated 1481, in which the text reads 'the 22nd year of Tiberius.'"[36]

But both of those finds pale in comparison to the reports of David W. Beyer in 1996. After combing through the collections of the Library of Congress and British Library he found that both the 1481 and 1517 copies of the Latin *Antiquities of the Jews* support the "22nd year of Tiberius" reading. On top of that, he went on to show that *thirty-one other editions* dating back to the twelfth century also support that reading. Most importantly, he demonstrated that the *1544 printing of Antiquities in Basel* was the moment when the date of Philip's death was changed due to a scribal error! He writes, "Unfortunately, this Greek edition was destined to become the universally accepted standard by the highest echelons of the scholastic world even though its chronology of Philip and Herod was divergent to all previously recorded histories."[37] The classic English translation of Josephus by William Whiston, which was used by scholars for centuries and is what is read by most English people even today, is based off of this faulty Greek edition!

While Beyer's recent find is extraordinarily interesting, the fact is that there still are other manuscripts that exist prior to the 1544 printing fiasco that also back the 4 BC dating. So while the "scribal error" in Basel is a very important find and something to be brought up in discussion, it not definitive proof for the 1 BC date. It simply means there is great ambiguity in these texts and we should rely on other factors outside of Josephus to validate either the early or late figure in Josephus' texts.

Besides Scripture's own chronology and the reasonableness of Josephus' original work supporting a 1 BC date, another reason to reject the 4 BC date is the *near unanimous testimony* of the early church fathers. Irenaeus of Lyon, Clement of Alexandria, Tertullian of Carthage, Origen of Alexandria, Julius Africanus, Eusebius of Caesarea, Epiphanius of Salamis, Hippolytus of Thebes, and other ancient church church fathers, bishops, and historians *all give the date of 3/2 BC for Christ's birth.* Jack Finegan, a late 20th century expert in biblical chronology who believes Christ was born in 2 BC, writes, "there is a remarkable consensus of the nine most important authorities for the year 3/2 B.C."[38] Do we know better than all of these early church authorities? Some of whom were removed from the time of Christ by only a couple generations? Besides the fathers' testimony, how could the historian tasked with setting up the current dating system in the sixth century, Dionysius Exiguus, get the birth of Christ so wrong? Well, I don't believe he did. He was only a year and a half off, not six or seven years!

Summarizing why I believe 1 BC appears to be the most reasonable date for Herod's death: (1) the date of the beginning of John's ministry and the age Jesus entered ministry support the 'late date' for Herod's death, (2) the 'late date' fits perfectly with Jesus being thirty-three and a half years old on April 3, AD 33 which is one of the two possible dates for His crucifixion, (3) Jesus' preaching of judgment upon the temple and Jerusalem began in AD 30— Jesus said the destruction of the temple and end of the age would happen in His generation (Matt. 24:34)—this gives an even forty years (a generation) from the time of the preaching of judgment to the fulfillment of that judgment and "days of vengeance" (Luke 21:22)—the apostolic generation was truly given a full forty years of warning to repent before their 'harlot city' Jerusalem was brought to complete destruction, (4) Josephus is not always reliable when it comes to assigning dates to kings, (5) concerning the date of Herod's death in Josephus there are multiple manuscripts that disagree with one another and it is very plausible 1 BC was the original reading, (6) the reigns of Josephus' sons were back-dated as convincingly demonstrated by the recent research of Steinmann and Young, (7) the witness of the early church father's is near unanimous for the 'late date' of Herod's death, and (8) the astronomical signs in the heavens that fit the description of Matthew 2 fit within the timeframe of the later date.

While triple conjunctions between Jupiter and Regulus or Jupiter and Venus have occurred before, what happened in the sky from 3-2 BC was *completely unprecedented*. AS Haley reminds us that the type of conjunction that occurred between Jupiter and Venus happens every 144 years while the triple conjunctions between Jupiter and Regulus happen once every 83 years. He goes on to say, "the periodicity of the two cycles will repeat once about every (=83 X 144) 11,952 years. And that is without regard to the second closer conjunction with Venus, to within 30 arc seconds, which would have been seen only once in about every 1,090 years. Because 144 is commensurate with 2,160 (= 2 X 1,080 = 15 X 144), we could expect the unique course of planetary events seen in 3-2 B.C. to recur again in about 179,280 (= 15 X 11, 952) years."[39] *This event was not simply rare, it has only ever happened once.* Reserved to herald the birth of our Lord!

Not only was this journey of Jupiter *completely unprecedented* and likely never to be repeated, but as we've already seen, the night Jesus was born also witnessed *the brightest star* recorded in history. This is the *primary reason* the conjunction between Jupiter and Venus on June 17, 2 BC is shown in secular planetariums all over the world. Interestingly, very early Christian witness also testifies to an extremely bright star the night of Christ's birth. Ignatius, who knew John the son of Zebedee, wrote, "A star shone forth in heaven brighter than all the stars; its light was indescribable and its strangeness caused amazement."[40] While the Bible makes no mention that the star of Bethlehem was brighter than all the other stars, the 'Jupiter Hypothesis' confirms this early Christian testimony.

It is possible Ignatius could have been referring to a supernova that had been shining for 150 years in the constellation of Coma ('Desired'). Coma/Desired is one of the three 'decan constellations' in Virgo/Virgin. This first decan depicts a woman holding a child. Bullinger refers to a 13th century Arab Christian historian named Abulfaragius who said that "Zoroaster, or Zerdusht, the Persian, was a pupil of Daniel the Prophet, and that he predicted to the Magianns (who were the astronomers of Persia), that when they should see *a new star* appear it would notify the birth of a mysterious child, whom they were to adore. It is further stated in the *Zend Avesta* that this new star was to appear in the sign of the Virgin."[41] The bright supernova in the *'Woman and Child' constellation in Virgo* sang with the brightest star in recorded history (the Venus/Jupiter conjunction) to make the night of Christ's birth *one special night.*

Christians should be in awe over the star that led the great Persian court counselors to Jesus—for it was intentionally and intricately designed by the Word Himself on Day 4 of creation to one day lead others to Him the night He would be born for the world's salvation. At the same time, we must recognize that the 'signs' in the heavens are part of the *old creation age*. The 'signs' in the heavens were part of the "elementary principles of the world" that are now fulfilled in Christ (Gal. 4:1-11; Col. 2:16-23; Heb. 8:13). The heavenly signs in their uncorrupted form were a prophetic witness of the coming Deliverer. In their purest form, the Mazzaroth and all the constellations within the Mazzaroth, testify beautifully about the Gospel. Why? Because God was the Artist who crafted every constellation and bestowed on them all their ancient names and symbolic meaning (Job 38:32).

While there are plenty of modern works on this subject, a classic that still stands tall is E. W. Bullinger's *The Witness of the Stars*. Bullinger built off of other great works like *Mazzaroth* by Frances Rolleston and *The Gospel in the Stars* by Joseph Seiss. Bullinger writes, "These pictures were designed to preserve, expound, and perpetuate the one first great promise and prophecy of Gen. 3:15, that all hope for Man, all hope for Creation was bound up in *a Coming Redeemer*."[42] The progression from revelation in the heavens to revelation in Scripture really follows the structure of Psalm 19. It progresses from *natural revelation*—"The heavens declare the glory of God...night unto night reveals knowledge"—to written revelation—"the law of the LORD is perfect, converting the soul" (Psalm 19:1-11). From *partial knowledge* to *perfect knowledge*. The uncorrupted ancient message of the heavens, and the 'school of Daniel', was simply *an explanation of the Gospel of Jesus Christ*. (Many have built off the work of Rolleston and Seiss in expounding this cosmological Gospel.)

In the new day Christ has brought about we are no longer under the signs of old creation. Those signs brilliantly served their purpose and were brought to an end in Christ just like man's tutelage under angels was brought to an end in Christ. While we should be in awe about what *the uncorrupted Gospel message of the Mazzaroth signifies*, we must also know that even the Mazzaroth has significant *vanishing moments*. For instance, Bullinger points out that the important 'cross constellation' in Libra vanished from the eyes of those who dwelt in Jerusalem around the time of Christ's sacrifice. This cross *prophetically spoke* of the Coming Messiah's 'finished work'. Bullinger writes, "The Southern Cross was just visible in the latitude of Jerusalem at the time of the first coming of our Lord to die. Since then, through the gradual recession of the Polar Star, it has not been seen in northern latitudes. It gradually disappeared and became invisible at Jerusalem when the Real Sacrifice was offered there. ... Dante sang of 'the four stars never beheld but by the early race of men.'"[43]

The Mazzaroth has one purpose—*to point people to Jesus*. It has served that purpose. Don't go looking to the stars in the sky for some sort of 'spiritual sign' that will enrich your life under modern day corrupt forms of astrology. That is evil. Also, don't get caught up in 'blood moon hysteria' in certain Christian circles that comes around every decade or so. Instead, simply appreciate how the greatest sign in the old creation age ('the star of Bethlehem') has pointed us to the Daystar of new creation ('Jesus'). Jesus is the only One we need to *gaze upon*. Jesus is the only One we need to *follow*. To go back to the stars and try to discern 'new messages' to direct us in the future would be like the Galatians who were going back to the "weak and beggarly elements" of the world (Gal. 4:9).[43] Those were "good" and "holy" *for their particular dispensation*, but we need them no more.

In conclusion, explorations on the meaning of the star as related to the birth of Christ are in the very beginning of a *golden era*. What modern astronomical software has allowed us to see can be a great *evangelistic tool*. It can help us defend the historicity of the Gospel accounts. It also can help us explore *the theological depths* of Christ's 'tabernacling among' us on the day of 'temple rededication'. This, of course, is only one of the many great wonders of the Christmas story and the dawn of the new day in Christ Jesus our Lord!

Appendix B
"The Nicene Creed"

We believe in one God, the Father almighty, maker of heaven and earth, of all things visible and invisible.

And in one Lord Jesus Christ, the only Son of God, begotten from the Father before all ages, God from God, Light from Light, true God from true God, begotten, not made; of the same essence as the Father. Through him all things were made. For us and for our salvation he came down from heaven; he became incarnate by the Holy Spirit and the virgin Mary, and was made human. He was crucified for us under Pontius Pilate; he suffered and was buried. The third day he rose again, according to the Scriptures. He ascended to heaven and is seated at the right hand of the Father. He will come again with glory to judge the living and the dead. His kingdom will never end.

And we believe in the Holy Spirit, the Lord, the giver of life. He proceeds from the Father and the Son, and with the Father and the Son is worshiped and glorified. He spoke through the prophets. We believe in one holy catholic and apostolic church. We affirm one baptism for the forgiveness of sins. We look forward to the resurrection of the dead, and to life in the world to come. Amen.

Published by the Christian Reformed Church
(https://www.crcna.org/welcome/beliefs/creeds/nicene-creed)

143

Works Cited

1. John Chrysostom. "Homilies on the Epistle to the Hebrews." *The Faith of the Early Fathers (Volume 2)*, ed. and trans. by William A. Jurgens, (Collegeville, MN.: Liturgical Press, 2007), 124.

2. Randy Alcorn. "Shepherd Status," in *Come, Thou Long-Expected Jesus*, Nancy Guthrie, Editor (Wheaton, IL: Crossway Books, 2008), pp. 85-89.

3. Michael Pomazansky, *Orthodox Dogmatic Theology*, trans. Seraphim Rose (Platina, CA: St. Herman of Alaska Brotherhood, 1983), 60.

4. Those interested in the historical veracity of the 'Shroud of Turin' and whether the imprint it bears truly resembles the 'Pantocrator' should watch "A Remarkable Relic Of The Resurrection" with Fr Robert Spitzer. For a short but thorough and up to date investigation of the shroud, read *The Turin Shroud: Physical Evidence of Life After Death?* by Mark Niyr.

5. James B. Jordan, *The Handwriting on The Wall* (Powder Springs, GA: American Vision, 2007), 220.

6. St. Ephraim the Syrian, *Hymns and Homilies of St. Ephraim the Syrian*, trans. J. T. Sarsfield Stopford (Veritatis Splendor Publications), 200, 221.

7. St. Ephraim the Syrian, *Hymns and Homilies*, 212.

8. St. Ephraim the Syrian, *Hymns and Homilies*, 179.

9. Bernard of Clairvaux, *Sermons for Advent and the Christmas Season*, trans. Irene Edmonds, Wendy Mary Beckett, and Conrad Greenia (Collegeville, MN.: Liturgical Press, 2007), 87.

10. Bernard of Clairvaux, "On the Joy His Birth Should Inspire," in *Sermons of St Bernard on Advent and Christmas: Including the Famous Treatise on the Incarnation Called 'Missus Est,'*, trans. St. Mary's Convent in York (London: R. & T. Washbourne Ltd., 1909), 75-77.

11. Bernard of Clairvaux, *Sermons for Advent and the Christmas Season*, 59.

12. Bernard of Clairvaux, *Sermons for Advent and the Christmas Season*, 101.

13. Martin Luther, *Sermons of Martin Luther, volume 1*, edited by John Nicholas Lenker (Grand Rapids, MI: Baker Book House, 1983), 133.

14. Martin Luther, *Martin Luther's Christmas Book*, edited by Roland H. Bainton (Minneapolis, MN: Fortress Press, 2017), 36.

15. Martin Luther, *The Sermons of Martin Luther, volume 1*, trans. John Lenker (Minneapolis, MN: All Lands Press, 1906), 134-160.

16. Luther, *Martin Luther's Christmas Book*, 35.

17. Luther, *Martin Luther's Christmas Book*, 30.

18. Luther, *Martin Luther's Christmas Book*, 51.

19. Luther, *Martin Luther's Christmas Book*, 33.

20. E. Stanley Jones, *A Song of Ascents: A Spiritual Autobiography* (Nashville, TN: Abingdon Press, 1968), 98.

21. Phillips Brooks, "O Little Town of Bethlehem", 1868.

22. Bernard of Clairvaux, *Sermons for Advent and the Christmas Season*, 93.

23. Martin Luther, *Martin Luther's Christmas Book*, 44.

24. While Rick Larson's popular presentation of the 'Jupiter Hypothesis' is by and large *very helpful*, it does have a few weaknesses. (This is one reason I have written a whole appendix on the subject rather than just telling people to go watch his documentary.) One of the film's weaknesses is that Larson assumes the 'Jupiter Hypothesis' was made possible because of the Copernican Revolution and mathematical insights of Kepler. This is simply not true. It matters not whether one is a geocentrist or a heliocentrist. Also, the mathematical insights are more dependent on the geocentrist Tycho-Brahe than the heliocentrist Kepler. In

fact, present day Neo-Tychonists (like Gerardus Bouw of *Case Western University*) hold to the 'Jupiter Hypothesis' without contradicting their own cosmological model. While Bouw (for unconvincing reasons) does not believe the 'star of Bethlehem' was the journey of the planet Jupiter and prefers the theory of angel or special miracle, he still believes Jupiter was "a sign" the magi observed and that it "heralded" the birth of Jesus. (Gerardus D. Bouw, "The Star of Bethlehem." *The Biblical Astronomer*, Vol. 8, No. 86, p. 12, Fall 1998). A second major weakness with Larson's film is that he makes too bold of claims about both Philo and Josephus. If he was a little more nuanced in handling the disputed nature of his claims, and was able to bolster his defense with other sources, I believe even more skeptics would be convinced of the 'Jupiter Hypothesis'. This is one reason I will be taking time in this appendix to defend the 'late date' of Herod's death. Larson's defense is partially inaccurate and partially too simplistic—this gives more ammo to skeptics. Having said this, these mistakes should in no way discourage anyone from watching what otherwise is a fantastic visual introduction to the 'Jupiter Hypothesis'.

25. See the articles "Other Evidence for the Date of the Nativity", "When Herod Ruled - Resolving the Dates", and "The Star of Bethlehem and the Nativity" at accurmudgeon.blogspot.com.

26. Philo, *Every Good Man Is Free*. See http://www.earlyjewishwritings.com/text/philo/book33.html, 74.

27. AS Haley. "The Star of Bethlehem and the Nativity." https://accurmudgeon.blogspot.com/2009/10/star-of-bethlehem-and-nativity.html. Accessed December 16, 2021.

28. Ernest Martin, *The Star of Bethlehem: The Star that Astonished the World (Second Edition)* (Portland, OR: The Associates for Scriptural Knowledge, 2003), https://www.askelm.com/star/star004.htm.

29. Martin, https://www.askelm.com/star/star004.htm.

30. Peter Leithart, *The Four* (Moscow, ID: Canon Press, 2010), 44.

31. Victor Wierwille, *Jesus Christ Our Promised Seed* (Knoxville, OH: American Christian Press, 1982), 63-64.

32. Paulus Orosius, *The Seven Books of History Against the Pagans*, VI.22 and VII.2.

33. Jack Finegan, *Handbook of Biblical Chronology Revised Edition* (Peabody, MA: Hendrickson, 1998), 306.

34. Flavius Josephus, *Antiquities of the Jews*, 17.41-45.

35. Andrew E. Steinmann and Rodger C. Young, "Evidences That Herod the Great's Sons Antedated Their Reigns to a Time before Herod's Death", http://www.rcyoung.org/articles/Antedating.pdf. Accessed December 17th, 2021.

36. W.E. Filmer, "The Chronology of the Reign of Herod the Great", JTS 17 (1966), 283-98.

37. David W. Beyer, "Josephus Reexamined: Unraveling the Twenty-Second Year of Tiberius", in Jerry Vandaman (ed.), *Chronos, Kairos, Christos II: Chronological, Nativity, and Religious Studies in Memory of Ray Summers* (Macron, GA: Mercer University Press, 1998), 86-87.

38. Finegan, *Handbook of Biblical Chronology Revised Edition*, 291.

39. AS Haley. "The Star of Bethlehem and the Nativity." https://accurmudgeon.blogspot.com/2009/10/star-of-bethlehem-and-nativity.html. Accessed December 16, 2021.

40. Ignatius of Antioch, *The Apostolic Fathers*, trans. Michael W. Holmes (Baker Academic, 2006), 101.

41. E. W. Bullinger, *The Witness of the Stars* (Grand Rapids, MI: Kregel, reprint of the 1893 ed.), 37.

42. Bullinger, *The Witness of the Stars*, 19.

43. Bullinger, *The Witness of the Stars*, 48.

44. See Peter Leithart's book *Delivered from the Elements of the World* for more on 'the flesh', 'circumcision', and 'the elements of the world'.

Artwork Cited

Cover. Daniel Bonnell. *Seeing Shepherds*. 2011, oil on canvas. https://bonnellart.com/digital-paintings/seeing-shepherds-28x36-oil-on-canvas. Used with permission.

1. Francesco Guarino. The Meeting of Zechariah and Elizabeth. 17th century. Oil on Canvas. https://commons.wikimedia.org/wiki/File:The_Meeting_of_Zechariah_and_Elizabeth_).jpg. Public domain.

2. Alexandr Ivanov. Archangel Gabriel struck dumb Zachariah. Wikimedia Commons, Wikimedia Foundation, https://commons.wikimedia.org/wiki/File:Alexandr_Ivanov_010.jpg. Public domain.

3. Henry Ossawa Tanner. Study for the Annunciation, ca. 1898, oil on wood, Smithsonian American Art Museum, Gift of Mr. and Mrs. Norman Robbins, 1983.95.187. https://americanart.si.edu/artwork/study-annunciation-23684. Public domain.

4. Unknown artist. Wall painting of the Visitation from Timios Stavros Church in Pelendi, Cyprus. 14th-century. https://commons.wikimedia.org/wiki/File:Visitation_Pelendri.jpg. Public domain.

5. Anselm Feuerbach. Miriam. https://commons.wikimedia.org/wiki/File:Feuerbach_Mirjam_2.jpg. Public domain.

6. James Tissot. David Singing and Playing the Harp. 1896-1902. Gouache on board. The Jewish Museum, New York. Public Domain.

7. Gaetano Gandolfi. Joseph's Dream. https://commons.wikimedia.org/wiki/File:%27Joseph%27s_Dream%27,_painting_by_Gaetano_Gandolfi,_c._1790.jpg. Public domain.

8. Unknown artist. 13th-century Byzantine Mosaic from Chora Church in Istanbul, Turkey. https://www.wikiart.org/en/byzantine-mosaics/journey-to-bethlehem-mosaic-1320. Public domain.

9. Barna Da Siena. The Birth of Jesus. 14th-century. http://www.sviewp.com/Images/Mary-Swaddling%20Clothes.jpg. Public Domain.

10. This is the text and a scan of the actual, original, first printing of the 1611 King James Version, the 'HE' Bible, for John Chapter 1. https://www.kingjamesbibleonline.org/John-Chapter-1_Original-1611-KJV/. Public domain.

11. Daniel Bonnell. *Seeing Shepherds*. 2011, oil on canvas. https://bonnellart.com/digital-paintings/seeing-shepherds-28x36-oil-on-canvas. Used with permission.

12. Unknown artist. The Gospel from Mokvi, 1300. https://commons.wikimedia.org/wiki/File:Genealogy_of_Christ_(part)_(The_Mokvi_Four_Gospels_1300).jpg. Public domain.

13. Marc Chagall, The sacrifice of Isaac, 1966, Oil on canvas, 230x235 cm, Musee national Message Biblique Marc Chagall, Nice. http://assaffeller.com/presentations/Marc%20Chagall,%20Crucifixion%201/Slide43.JPG.

14. Circumcision of Christ, Menologion of Basil II, 979-984. Public domain.

15. Arent de Gelder. Simeon's Song of Praise. https://commons.wikimedia.org/wiki/File:Aert_de_Gelder_-_Het_loflied_van_Simeon.jpg. Public domain.

16. Rembrandt. *Simeon and Anna in the Temple*. 1627, oil on oak wood. https://commons.wikimedia.org/wiki/File:Rembrandt_

Simeon_and_Anna_in_the_Temple@Kunsthalle_Hamburg.jpg.
Public domain.

17. Josefa de Óbidos. The Sacrificial Lamb. between circa 1670
and circa 1684, oil on canvas. https://commons.wikimedia.org/
wiki/File:Josefa_de_Ayala_-_The_Sacrificial_Lamb_-
_Walters_371193.jpg. Public domain.

18. Giuseppe Arcimboldo. Head of Herod. circa 1566, painting.
https://commons.wikimedia.org/wiki/File:Giuseppe_
Arcimboldo_Herod.jpg. Public domain.

19. Josef Langl Blick. Blick auf Betlehem bei Nacht. https://
commons.wikimedia.org/wiki/File:Josef_Langl_Blick_
auf_Bethlehem_bei_Nacht.jpg. Public domain.

20. Spicer, William Ambrose. Our day in the light of prophecy
and providence. https://commons.wikimedia.org/wiki/
File:Our_day_in_the_light_of_prophecy_and_providence_(1921)_
(14590752108).jpg. Public domain.

21. Breslevmeir. חנוכה. https://commons.wikimedia.org/wiki/
File:חנוכה.jpg.

22. Edward Burne-Jones. The Star of Bethlehem. 1885/1890,
watercolor and bodycolor with scraping on ten sheets. https://
commons.wikimedia.org/wiki/File:Edward_Burne-Jones_-
_The_Star_of_Bethlehem_-_Google_Art_Project.jpg. Public
domain.

23. Eugène Girardet. Flight into Egypt. Oil on Canvas. https://
commons.wikimedia.org/wiki/
File:Eugène_Girardet,_Flight_into_Egypt.jpg. Public domain.

24. William Hole. Jesus Amidst The Doctors In The Temple.
https://commons.wikimedia.org/wiki/File:William_Hole_Jesus_

Amidst_The_Doctors_In_The_Temple_400.jpg. Public domain.

25. Fritz von Uhde. Christmas Night. Oil on canvas. https://commons.wikimedia.org/wiki/File:Fritz_von_Uhde_Heilige_Nacht.jpg. Public domain.

26. Unknown Artist. St Nicholas slaps Arius. Fresco of the Council of Nicea, Sümela Monastery. https://commons.wikimedia.org/wiki/File:St_Nicholas_slaps_Arius.jpg. Public domain.

27. Unknown Artist. Christ Pantocrator (Sinai). Saint Catherine's Monastery, Sinai (Egypt). 6th Century, encaustic. https://commons.wikimedia.org/wiki/File:Christ_Icon_Sinai_6th_century.jpg. Public domain.

28. Louisa Anne. Choir singing on Christmas Day. 1887. https://commons.wikimedia.org/wiki/File:Choir_singing_on_Christmas_Day_by_Louisa_Anne_(née_Stuart),_Marchioness_of_Waterford.jpg. Public domain.

29. François Vincent Latil. Bernard of Clairvaux d'apres Philippe de Champaign. 17th century, oil on canvas. https://commons.wikimedia.org/wiki/File:Saint_Bernard_Philippe_de_Champaigne_(d%27après)_Saint_Etienne_du_Mont.jpg. Public domain.

30. William Blake. Jacob's Dream. 1805, pen and ink and water color. https://commons.wikimedia.org/wiki/File:Blake_jacobsladder.jpg. Public domain.

31. James Tissot. Nicodemus. between 1886 and 1894, gouache over graphite on gray wove paper. https://commons.wikimedia.org/wiki/File:Brooklyn_Museum_-_Nicodemus_(Nicodème)_-_James_Tissot_-_overall.jpg. Public domain.

Made in the USA
Las Vegas, NV
04 December 2022

61149848R00085